St. Andrew Convent

Fragments of My Life

Books by Catherine de Hueck Doherty:

POUSTINIA

THE GOSPEL WITHOUT COMPROMISE

NOT WITHOUT PARABLES

SOBORNOST

STRANNIK

I LIVE ON AN ISLAND

DEAR FATHER

OUR LADY'S UNKNOWN MYSTERIES

THE PEOPLE OF THE TOWEL AND WATER

Early Works:

FRIENDSHIP HOUSE (1946)

DEAR BISHOP (1947)

WHERE LOVE IS, GOD IS (1952)

Fragments of My Life

Catherine de Hueck Doherty

Ave Maria Press • Notre Dame, Indiana 46556

Library of Congress Catalog Card Number: 79-56889
International Standard Book Number: 0-87793-193-3 (Cloth)
0-87793-194-1 (Paper)

© 1979 by Ave Maria Press, Notre Dame, Indiana 46556

Cover design and layout: Joyce Stanley

Printed and bound in the United States of America.

Contents

Introduction

Why should I write *Fragments of My Life?* Do you, dear friends, have any idea? I know what those of you who know me, my friends, will say: "Well, Katie, of course you should write about your life. It will be fun. Like the comics! We had some really exciting days! We could read it to the children!" That's what the Harlem people would say.

And those I lived with in the slums—the Poles, the Ukrainians—what would they say about these *Fragments?* They would wink while they offered me some homemade wine, and they would say: "Now Katerina, don't prevaricate! Make it truthful! You're a storyteller and you just can't help it! Not that you varnish the truth, but by the time it comes out in print it will really look fantastic! Something quite simple, like giving a party for your child, develops into a fairy tale. You just can't touch anything without making it colorful like we do in Poland and in Russia. You're an ethnic all right. On the other hand, why shouldn't you tell it like a story? So many biographies are truthful but dull!" That's what the Toronto people whom I knew in the slums would say.

What would my honorable intellectual friends say, the many, many wonderful people I have met in universities all over the world? They certainly would say: "Indeed, Catherine, you should write your autobiography. You have led a very interesting life, a historical life. You've been part of very strange events. You've had many adventures. Somewhere along the line you 'got religion.' True, there is an abundance of religious autobiographies, but considering that you lecture with verve and simplicity, and that you can appeal to both the intellectual and the *hoi polloi,* we don't see why you shouldn't write about your life."

Then there are the publishers. They want a follow-up to *Tumbleweed,* my biography written by my late husband Eddie before we were married in 1943. It sort of stops on the day we were married. Much has happened since.

Truthfully, and against the advice of my good friends, I'm not too keen about writing this. But perhaps I should write it if for no other reason than this: No one else can write about my life as I can! It has too many faces, too many facets.

But I want to warn my readers that it will be a strange piece of writing because the stories and chapters are not necessarily chronological. And I'm a born storyteller, easily enchanted with ordinary things, often seeing people as they really are, not as they appear to be. I'm used to endowing all life with magic and wonder and mystery.

Yes, that's the kind of story it will be—fragments from the life of a Russian storyteller who reveals truth as it is revealed to her.

So, dear reader and friend, do not consider this book an autobiography, far from it. It is a woman looking over her life and writing down little *vignettes,* or *essays,* if you want to call it by a more accurate name! But all it is, really, is a book of memories that wander from my childhood to my youth, to middle age and old age, and then come back again.

You know I am in love with God, and this is a fact. But if you are in love with God you are also in love with people; one follows the other like night follows day and day follows night! Thus I am in love with all of you, with all those who read this book. When you are in love you want to share, and in these humble pages I simply share with you, my dear friends (known and unknown), part of my life. Over my many years in the apostolate, many of you have shared your lives with me. I share it lovingly, for I do love you.

Catherine de Hueck Doherty
Madonna House, Combermere,
Ontario

Catherine's father

. . . and mother

1. Earliest Memories Over Kvass

I was born in a pullman car. My mother, having come to the Great Fair at Nijni-Novgorod (now Gorki) miscalculated, and I was born on the train. Worried about my catching a disease, she had me baptized on the same day, which was the feast of our Lady's Assumption. I was baptized in the Russian Orthodox church, there being no Roman Catholic church in the city at that time.

Being born means having a family. As far as I know, from all the stories told me, I had a wonderful family dating back to the 11th century. My ancestors were farmers in the district of Tombov, south of Moscow. Their name was Kolyschkine. The word "kol" means "boundary peg." Maybe some of my ancestors were surveyors. Later, somewhere along the line, my great-grandfather received titles of nobility from the Tsar. As far as I was concerned, this didn't matter very much: I was delighted to be a descendant of farmers.

Another daughter, Natasha, had been born before me, but she died in infancy. After my birth there followed three sons. They were all miscarried. My parents, of course, were sad at their deaths, and wept over them very much. They were all baptized. Then there were two younger brothers—Serge who was born in Egypt, and Andrew who was born in Russia when I was about 16. I got to know both of them very well.

My first memory is a very lovely one. I used to love a certain park, my mother later told me. And in this park was a pond into which bright red leaves kept falling. I was eternally running after these red leaves to catch them. On one occasion, in order to do so, I just walked right into the pond! This presented considerable difficulties for my nanny!

I was a person of early "philosophical" inclinations. I liked discussions. My father didn't mind this too much since he only had to deal with me at lunch and dinner! But mother used to get a little impatient. Let me illustrate.

Electricity finally came to our home. Now for a five-year-old, electricity is quite something. I noticed a little button. When you pushed it, lots of light! Instead of all those oil lamps that took a while to light—*boom!* the light came on. This delighted me. So, I kept pushing the switch up and down, up and down. Of course, that wasn't very good for the electrical system in those days, so my mother forbade me to do it. The miracle of light was indeed a miracle to me.

Now, I wasn't disobedient! On the contrary, I was very obedient—but I liked to argue. When mother forbade me to push the button I sat down in father's big chair. I asked mother: "Why can't I push those little buttons to make the light go on?" And mother answered, "Because I said so."

That was a very wrong answer for me. Remember, I had metaphysical leanings! "Only God can say things like that," I pointed out to her. "You can't say things like that. You want me to clean my dolls every day so they will be tidy. Well, if I say I don't want to clean my dolls because I don't want to clean them, what would you do?" She said: "I would do what I am going to do this very minute." She took me by the hand and put me in a corner! That was my punishment.

With my nose between two walls, I cogitated—philosophized! I must have been there 15 minutes when mother called, "You can come out now." I said, "I haven't finished thinking." So she left me there. Finally I was ready. I said, "Mother, I think I'll go to grandmother's house. I don't feel comfortable around here!" or words to that effect. "Furthermore," I said, "you can have my dolls!"

Grandmother lived about five blocks away—quite a distance in those days for a five-year-old. I went to grandmother and said, "Do you think mother feels sorry that she let me go?" Grandmother was smart. She answered, "She feels very sad, and this is stupid on your part." "Yes, it looks like it, doesn't it?" I walked back home.

What can I say? The years I spent in Ekaterinoslav were like that. You could paint pictures of a little girl wading into a pond to catch red leaves in the fall; you could draw a sullen little figure with her hands in her pockets, very sure of herself, walking to grandmother's house; you could draw a little girl standing in a corner, her nose between two walls, thinking hard and coming to world-shattering conclusions. I think in pictures. I can't help it, that's the way I am.

One day father announced that we were leaving for Turkey. My governess got a map out to show me where it was. We took the train south for Turkey.

Do you know the thrill of traveling on a train when you are five? Oh, what a joy! It excites your curiosity.

On one occasion I got lost on the train because I went to find the engine. I met the engineer and found out that the train was fueled by burning wood. I was so sad I almost cried. I said: "You mean you cut our beautiful trees for those engines and put them into those big fires? God doesn't like that." Evidently the engineer was a Christian, for he patiently explained to me: "Of course God likes it. He gave us the earth and the trees and everything else to use for our needs." We had a wonderful talk. (I didn't understand half of it, or even one quarter, but it was nice.) Finally, the nanny came and practically spanked me because she had gone through the whole train and couldn't find me!

Well, I got to be friends with the conductors. They were always giving me kvass, a lightly fermented drink made from bread. I liked it. So, they would say, crooking their little fingers, "Just drop in anytime." I did drop in anytime, and had some kvass. Those journeys were long, and you had to be a child to enjoy them.

Odessa is a port city and I, who had never seen the sea before, beheld it in all its glory. It took me days to recover from the shock of so much beauty. I saw ships and clapped my hands with delight. I asked my father, "Did God make them all?" My father looked at me and said, "Well, God made the men and gave them skills. Then the men made the boats. Yes, God made the boats." (A little metaphysical question well answered by father.)

From Odessa we took a ship to Istanbul. I used to go up to the deckhands and tap them on the knees, which was the only part of them I could reach. I would say, "Aren't you happy you are a God-man?" Now that I look back at my behavior, I see that I must have left a trail of astonished people behind me!

11

I got to know the captain of the boat. When nobody was looking, I just walked up the many stairs that led to his house (that's the fastest way to get to know a captain!). I could spell but it took me a little while to read "Captain." I knocked at the door very politely and a man called, "Come in." I said, "Hello, how do you do? God bless you." He said, "God bless you too. How do you do? Are you one of my passengers?" I said, "I don't know what 'passengers' means. I came to find out what 'Captain' means. You are so high up, like in a nest. Are you like a hen looking after all of us at night and during the day?"

He was chunky, a very nice man, and we became great friends. "Yes," he said, "I am like a hen, but you musn't call me that because I am not a hen. I'm a cock." "Ohhhh," I said, "I know you. You're Jar-Ptiza. I must bring you a book to read about it."

"Do that little thing," he said. We exchanged names. "Excuse me for barging in, but I might come again because you have such a beautiful view of the water. I want to see where the water goes. Good-bye," I said.

My father and mother were horrified. They said, "You don't just barge into the captain's cabin like that!" "I didn't barge in," I said, "I knocked."

After that we sat at the captain's table and became very friendly with him. I had a wonderful appetite and ate everything placed before me. Ordinarily that would have made me fat, except that I lost it all running around the ship. There wasn't a place on that ship I didn't explore.

We reached Istanbul where my father had some business, and we stayed for about a year.

While we were waiting to take possession of our house in the city—there being some unexplainable delay—we lived in a large, lovely villa. Nobody bothered me, so I had lots of fun examining everything. I had and still have a quality of wonderment. I wondered at the flowers which were so beautiful—the bougainvillea, the hibiscus, azaleas, and so many others.

Do you know what the castor oil seed looks like?

It's a beautiful little seed, black and white, but dangerous! A little English friend and I liked the seeds so well that we started eating them. When evening came round there were two very sick little people. We had eaten more than a handful, and the doctor was called in.

What can a doctor do against digested castor seeds? Not much. We suffered for three days. I am telling you, friends, never again did we play with castor seeds, no matter how nice looking they were.

A young English friend and his parents settled down in the same villa as my parents. This English boy could speak only English, whereas I could speak French, Russian, English, and a little bit of German. His parents wondered which of these languages their boy would pick up. My parents wondered if my English would improve. They made a wager, but both parties were doomed to disappointment. We both learned Arabic! From whom? From a little Arab friend.

I saw Istanbul from the shoulders of a very tall man. He was attached to the Embassy, and was perfectly reliable. Seeing the city from the shoulders of a tall man when you are little gives you an unusual perspective: You see mainly the tops of people's heads. The men wore red fezes in those days, with a red pom-pom. The ladies were all covered up, except for their eyes, which were either brown or black. You could tell if a woman was fat or thin only if the wind suddenly blew up her black dress.

The aristocracy had beautiful palaces and gardens. Because of his business, father was often invited to these places, and sometimes I got to go along. Frequently I would get lost, like the time I discovered a whole courtyard full of girls and began playing "Blind Man's Bluff" with them. My parents always had to search me out, but they never scolded me. Like most five-year-olds I found adults and their conversations rather dull.

From Turkey we went to Greece. I don't remember how long we stayed, but I remember being quite excited about Greece in my own fashion.

First, there were these fantastic statues with their broken arms and legs and people oohing and aahing in front of them all the time. Then there were the temples which touched something deep in my heart. I used to return again and again to look at Apollo and Venus and all those temples. Everything, just everything, was made out of marble. You walked on marble outside, and your bedroom floors inside were made of marble. It was a bit cold but beautiful. You just couldn't live in Greece as a young girl and not be enchanted by the statues and temples.

I used to run up and down the stairs in the amphitheatre while my governess knitted. She was always knitting it seemed to me. I made up a fantasy about her, that she knitted herself into her wool and couldn't get out of it! Well, I remember playing with stones in this amphitheatre. I made a train, and had little stones for my mother, father, and the engineer. We went on all sorts of trips, and even off the rails sometimes!

At meals back at the hotel the waiter always called me, in English, "my little Miss." I found out later how to say "little Miss" in Greek, and told him that he should use that. He did and I liked that very much.

I had to study, of course. I haven't mentioned that yet because it was unpleasant. I didn't want to take any lessons, but father insisted that mother should teach me Russian. I could speak Russian, but I couldn't write it. Russian is easy to speak but hard to write. I learned the alphabet and how to put words together.

There was one persistent problem in Greece: artists who wanted to paint my picture because of my hair. I had very, very beautiful streaked hair. One strand was gold, the other silver. My governess used to put her hands on top of her head and shoo these artists off like they were little dogs.

We left Greece and traveled directly from Athens to Alexandria, Egypt.

The first thing I said to my mother when she told me we were going to Egypt was, "Oh, are we going to see what Jesus Christ saw when he was a little boy in Egypt?" I knew about Jesus, but I didn't know too much about how he got to Egypt and what he did there. I was all set to see the place where he had lived.

We settled in what I always called "The House." It was located in a very pleasant location on a Mediterranean beach some distance from Ramleh, a suburb of Alexandria. It had marble porches with lime and orange trees growing alongside. There was a beautiful garden and I had a very nice room of which I was very fond. I had a governess and there were Italian chambermaids and Arab cooks. Here it was decided that I should go to a school for girls in Ramleh.

To be absolutely frank, I don't know what my father did. I wasn't interested. He associated with ambassadors and other important people and often gave beautiful dinners. He used to come

14

home in carriages drawn by six white-plumed horses. One thing I do remember clearly: I had to behave!

I was a very well-behaved girl. Morning, noon and night manners were drilled into me. Turkish manners, Arab manners, Greek manners. My father had a very fine way of explaining things to me. About manners he used to say: "Manners are politeness, and politeness is charity toward people."

Example. He would take a knife and he would put peas on it and say, "Look, I am putting peas on my knife and putting it into my mouth. Aren't you afraid I might cut myself?" "Oh, yes," I exclaimed, "I sure am."

He said, "Actions like that make other people nervous. That's impolite. That's uncharitable." So, I learned that manners are part of charity.

I went to school and it was fun. Every day a little boy came to the gate of "The House" with a little donkey. He took me to school which was only a mile or so away. All the while he kept singing a song that I still remember: *"Tali ya bata, an a male eh! Tali ya bata, an a male eh!"* He was about 13, and I was always afraid that he would fall asleep because he had such a sleepy face. I would ask him, "Are you falling asleep?" He would say, "No, only half asleep." That's what he would do—fall half asleep. To wake himself up he would sing his monotonous song over and over again, *"Tali ya bata, an a male eh!"* I never did find out what those words meant. Often I would fall asleep! But we always arrived safely at school.

I must have been six, going on seven, when all this was happening.

Regarding my schooling. I was a very simple person. I believed everything they told me. We used to play in St. Francis' Corner on the school grounds, and I devoured everything the nuns told me about St. Francis. One day I announced that I would be like him when I grew up. He has been my love ever since.

I was a good pupil. Languages came to me very easily, as well as reading, writing, and talking! I read rapidly and extensively. There was a Bibliotheque Rose which contained hundreds of books written especially for girls. Father gave me one of these books each week. He didn't quite believe that I could read so fast. One day I was returning a book to him and asked for another. The book I had finished was called Les Malheurs de Sophie, the tragedies of a young girl named Sophie who got into lots of trouble. Quite unexpectedly, father decided to quiz me about the book. I told him the whole story of *Les Malheurs de Sophie* from beginning to end. He was convinced. So was everybody else!

I also did well in zoology and botany because I was forever picking up flowers and bringing home all kinds of beasties that frightened my teachers and parents. I will give you one outstanding example. It was the day I picked up a scorpion (not knowing what it was) and my mother fainted. Now my mother was not the fainting type!

I saw these two, what appeared to me, crayfish, acting like two knights fighting in battle. They were out in the sun pushing each other around. (I later learned that they were two males fighting over a female, but I didn't know this at the time.) I watched them fighting. Finally, one of them killed the other with the needle in his tail. I got very angry and said, "I want to tell you something, you are going to prison." By God's grace (and through no expertise on my part), I grabbed him in the middle in such a way that his murderous tail could not touch me. Otherwise I could have been killed. I called out to mother, "Mother, we've got to do something to this character because he just killed his pal, his brother." When mother saw me with the scorpion, she passed out.

I shouted, and everybody came running. We gave mother some water. In the meantime, I had placed this little scorpion on the tabletop, and he was scampering all over it. The servants picked mother up and the waitresses screamed. I turned to the only sensible person there, the Arab cook, and said, "Sir, what are they shouting about?" He answered, "Little woman, what you have on the table is a scorpion, and they are very dangerous creatures. They can kill."

In those days I received high marks in arithmetic, but it didn't last. I never liked mathematics. As for geography, well, there is nothing better than traveling in order to get high marks in that subject.

The teacher wanted me to draw since art was part of the curriculum even in kindergarten. I asked her if I could write something instead. She said, "Certainly." So I wrote her the following story.

A little Arab boy walked into a marketplace one day. He had no father or mother. He was hoping somebody would give him something to eat, but nobody did. He was an honest little boy. His father and mother had taught him to live according to the Koran. The Koran forbids stealing, so he didn't steal any food. But at the end of the day he was very, very hungry. Not even the tourists gave him any *bakshish*—pennies that the children begged from them.

So he died. When he died our Lady herself came to take him home. (You know how the Muslims love our Lady. They call her Miriam.) Well, she took the little boy in her arms and started going up to heaven when halfway up they met Jesus Christ, the great prophet of the Koran. Together they took the little boy to God the Father. God the Father was so happy to see him. He gave him many fruits to eat, and the boy found little playmates just as it says in the Koran.

Do you know what happened to all the people who didn't give him anything? A terrible thing happened. All their wares were destroyed. Worms came into their food and it was ruined.

The teacher liked my story.

Speaking of playmates, I remember a little girl named Maria Papanicola. She was the daughter of the priest of the Greek Orthodox church which was right next to us. My mother was Orthodox, and she used to go there all the time. Maria and I became very friendly. She taught me Greek. But best of all, she was a playmate right next door.

Even in those early years, my predominant trait revealed itself. A kind of "religiosity," a sense of wonder. Everything was so wonderful, exciting, and interesting. A little later I developed an awareness of the poor. Around the age of nine I formed the habit of saying a Hail Mary for each poor person I met. I still do.

When God hits a little girl in her heart with these arrows, who can really tell what is happening? The little girl can.

age 8, with her mother,
in Egypt

1900, a baby picture

2. Growing Up in Egypt

I was doing very well at school until I broke one of the cardinal eating rules of Egypt. I knew that you could not eat dates or grapes without washing them in scalding water, but I didn't realize that the same rule applied to tangerines and oranges. These latter grew profusely in our garden, and it was tantalizing for a little one like me to hit my nose on them and not be able to eat them.

So one day I found myself holding a tangerine and biting into it. I seemed to be all right that day, but the next day—my God was I sick! I was so sick it wasn't funny! My parents became extremely worried. They got a doctor who said that I had amoebic dysentery. Even though father called in specialists from Alexandria, I started to sink fast. Thinking I was consoling my parents, I said, "You don't have to worry if I die. I am going to be with the angels and with little Jesus, and I am going to dance with all the saints. There are lots of children saints. I can write you letters from there. It's going to be fun."

I didn't realize that I just about thrust a sword through my mother's heart. I saw my father turn away a couple of times, with tears running down his face. I wasn't consoling anybody.

Our Arab cook came to my father and said, "Look, Sir, why don't you get an Arab doctor? He could cure this child." Father evidently had not thought about that, and got an Arab doctor right away. As far as I can remember, he prescribed pomegranate seeds. "Put them into alcohol, and let them ferment in the sun," he said. "Then give her this medicine four times a day on a teaspoon."

Miraculously I got well. The Arab doctor said: "Now the little mem-sahib should go to Europe. And, please, she must never eat anything that is not boiled."

Shortly after little "mem-sahib" departed with her mother for Switzerland to recuperate. We traveled much, and the skinny little thing that I was soon became the chubby little person I had been before. This incident put a real scare into my family, and I never again ate another tangerine in Egypt, unless it had been thoroughly boiled!

Another incident I remember concerned the belly dance. When I was around nine or ten I used to visit the Bedouins who came from the dunes of the desert. Once a year they put up their stands and sold their raw wool and beautiful handmade carpets. It was a time of rejoicing for them as well as us.

Near our house was an empty piece of land that didn't seem to belong to anyone. They asked to put up their tents there, and father said it didn't belong to him so they could avail themselves of it as far as he was concerned.

With my governess I visited those people. The Bedouin women did beautiful belly dancing. Now even as a little girl I had always been fond of dancing and had danced quite a bit. So with great excitement I used to sit with my governess and admire these beautiful women performing their dances. The different parts of their bodies seemed to be unconnected! They could move each breast separately, move their "behinds" separately, and move their bellies like undulating waves on the surface of the ocean. It was all very fascinating. Although I was little and didn't have any "protuberances," I did learn the belly dance. (Incidentally, at the school of Our Lady of Sion, I was also learning ballet and ballroom dancing as part of the curriculum.) Among the Bedouins the mothers and fathers were dancing also, and everything seemed perfectly decent. My governess didn't feel there was anything off-color about it, and neither did I. So I learned the belly dance.

One day my mother was entertaining at tea and she said, "Catherine, have you learned anything new in your dancing?" She wanted to exhibit me before her friends. I said, "Yes, I learned a new dance. I'll be right back." I lowered my skirt a little, and rolled up my blouse and I came back in and proceeded to perform the belly dance.

I'm telling you, my poor mother didn't know exactly what to do or say! She saw that I was totally innocent, so she allowed me to finish the dance. Then she said (her voice trembling slightly), "Where did you learn that one?" "From the Bedouins," I said.

A friend of my mother said, "Yes, I've seen this dance in the nightclubs of Paris." My mother said, "What is found in the nightclubs of Paris is performed in the open streets of Egypt." The result was that the ladies went to see for themselves. My mother never said anything very much to me about my belly dance, but she must have spoken to my governess, because I never visited the Bedouins again!

Every Easter, whenever possible, my father, mother and I, and later my brother Serge, used to go to Jerusalem for the Holy Week ceremonies. My mother was Orthodox, and she followed very carefully all the liturgies of the Orthodox Church. She especially liked the liturgy of the burial of Christ.

Father liked to bring home some of the olive oil from the Garden of Gethsemane. He had strong feelings about how everyone had abandoned Christ there; he often spoke about it. So in our house there always was a big quart bottle of this blessed oil from the Garden of Gethsemane. I inherited a great devotion to the passion of Christ from my father and mother.

One day my parents took me to the Rock of the Ascension, the place near Jerusalem from which Christ rose into heaven. I loved to look at that rock because it showed the imprints of a person who was standing on his toes on one foot, while the other was flat.

I had one ambition: to put my feet into these imprints of the feet of Christ. But that was a bit difficult, because they had this area cordoned off. But what's a rope to a little girl? One day I just slid underneath while everybody was praying, and put my little feet into those imprints, one up and the other down.

People began screaming, "Look what she's doing! Look what she's doing! Get that child out of there! Blasphemy, blasphemy!" A Russian priest came out and said, " 'Let the little children come to me,' have you forgotten that?" He helped me put my feet in the imprints of the feet of Jesus Christ, and then he escorted me out of there!

One day the cook came to my father and said, "Sir, you are a very good master and a very good man. Allah cannot continue to give you girls. Your next child will be a boy. It will be the blessing of Allah on you." Father secretly hoped that this blessing of the cook would come true. And so it did.

Serge was born in Egypt, in August, one of the hottest months there. During her pregnancy, mother hadn't been feeling too well, and everybody was praying for her. I was very interested in having a brother. Well, you should have seen the joy that reigned in the house at his birth. I don't remember, but my mother told me that the cook made a big feast. They had nonalcoholic drinks and dancing, and all because a boy was born.

But about nine months after Serge's birth, he contracted malaria, which is very easy to do in Egypt. For a year or so he was quite jaundiced.

Another time sickness struck my mother. She was infected with cholera during an epidemic, and hundreds of people were dying daily. The doctor came, took one look at her and said, "She's dying, she will die." My father wouldn't believe him, because father was a man of great faith. He had his own plan.

He called us all together—me and my little brother Serge who was still a babe in arms. With my mother totally naked, he brought in the wonderful oil from the Garden of Gethsemane and started anointing her from head to foot. First the hair, then the face, then the neck, then the breasts, right down to her toes. Then he turned her over and anointed her again in the same way. During all this time he asked us to pray, "Lord have mercy. Lord have mercy, Lord have mercy." (I still get gooseflesh when I think of this scene.)

After he finished, he covered her up and we all joined hands. He held the hand of the little baby and mine and my mother's. My mother, as far as I was concerned, was already dead. Then he blessed us all and said, "You can go to sleep now." The nurse told us later that he kept a vigil all night by my mother's side. He brought out an icon of the Blessed Mother and kept blessing our mother with it and saying, "Lord, have mercy on me a sinner. Save my wife."

In the morning we were brought in, about eleven o'clock, and mother was awake. She put her hands on my head and on my brother's head, blessed us, then fell asleep.

Within a few days—I don't remember how many—she was up and around! To get us all out of the city which was still infected with cholera, father organized a sort of safari to the desert near Cairo, complete with horses and mules. We stayed in a very primitive hotel where an artesian well provided pure, clear water. We stayed there quite a while, and mother improved. I remember how cold it was at night and how hot in the daytime. Eventually the cholera plague receded and we returned home to Alexandria.

I began menstruating fairly early in life. When this first happened to me mother said, "Oh, how lovely! Now you are a woman." "I am?" I asked. "Yes. You are a woman now. You can have babies. That's really exciting, isn't it! It's the most exciting thing that can happen to a woman in her life." Then she told me all about menstruation.

In the English language (years ago anyhow) some people used to call it "the curse." I never understood why. I never heard it spoken of as a curse. It was a blessing. "Now you can have babies." Mother said this so directly and so positively that I never asked any questions about how you get babies—at least, not then.

As always, we were very friendly with our servants, according to the customs of my people. More than friendly: We loved them.

One day the chief cook came to my father and asked permission for the little "mem-sahib" and her governess to attend his wedding. My father said, "But you are already married!" "Oh, yes," he said, "but unfortunately I am childless. Our spiritual guide agreed that I could take one more wife. And that's what I'm going to do. In fact, I have already invited the guests." My father gave his permission for me to attend with my governess.

Well, I never saw anything like it, and I don't think I ever will again! Even though my eyes were young, they opened to twice their size.

The first wife prepared the bridal chamber by fixing the bed, putting the garments out, and hanging garlands all around. I noticed also a delicious repast alongside the bed. The beautiful

23

ceremonies of the marriage began. I don't remember them exactly, but there were many exciting songs and legends and blessings of all kinds. Since I understood Arabic, I was able to enjoy everything. So I participated in a real Arab wedding which I will never forget—the singing, the dancing, the joy of it all, and the delicious food.

Arab women of that time were totally inconspicuous. All you could ever see were black bundles walking along, fat and thin. Everything, except for their eyes, was covered from head to foot. White veils hid their faces, and tubular contraptions on their noses further distorted their features.

My governess and I used to frequent the pasha's harem. He had a swimming pool that was my idea of heaven. The women disrobed quite naturally for their bath, while a eunuch sat in a corner reading his newspaper. As a eunuch, I guess, he was not interested in beholding those naked beauties. He never lifted his eyes.

The women swam and ate *rahat lucum* (Arab sweetmeats) with apparently no worries of getting fat. I met a very beautiful girl there, one of the concubines, and we became great friends. She was about 15, older than I, but we used to play together a great deal. It was fun to run around the pool and climb the balconies which were enclosed with lovely woodwork. We could play in the sun and never be seen from the outside.

Notwithstanding this enclosure, somehow a young man saw this beautiful girl and they fell in love. One day while we were playing together my friend said, "Here is a letter. A friend of mine will come and ask you for it when you go shopping today. Give it to him, but don't tell anybody, not even your governess. I trust you as my friend."

Sure enough, this gentleman approached me in the marketplace. He was one of the pasha's gardeners.

He said, "Little mem-sahib has a paper for me?"

I answered, "Yes, I have."

"Well," he said, "I'll give you one and I'll take one. The one I give you please place in her beautiful hands."

Well, I wasn't sure what he meant, so I asked, "Which beautiful hands? There are lots of beautiful hands."

"The ones that gave you the letter."

"Oh," I said, and I called her by name.

"But," he warned, "don't tell anybody. Keep it a secret."

"Yes," I promised, "it's a secret . . . fun . . . fun . . . fun!"

For a girl of nine or ten, this was truly a big adventure. Remember I was reading all kinds of books (like *Les Malheurs de Sophie*), and all kinds of exciting things like this happened to my heroines. Excited by the whole affair, I indeed kept my mouth shut.

When you come to think of it, those girls in the harem led a dull life! My governess told me that when the pasha wanted to "talk to one of them in the evening" (that's how she put it), he dropped his handkerchief near her. She picked it up and "went to talk to him." I don't know how well-informed my governess was, but that is what she told me.

Father had some business in the Sudan, so we took a trip there. Since the Nile flows through the Sudan as it does through Egypt, father thought it would be a good time for us to get acquainted with this wonderful and mysterious river. It proved to be a brilliant idea!

We traveled down the Nile in a flat-bottomed barge equipped with sails. It also had an engine in the back and carried all kinds of cargo. It stopped at almost every port, that's why father selected it. It was fun.

In those days, the Nile was a very dirty river. Gradually the waters became clearer and almost blue. I remember in places seeing huge leaves floating by. I think you could have sat on one of those leaves without drowning. In fact, whien we stopped at one place I asked father why I couldn't sit on a leaf like that. He said I might go under, and they didn't know how deep the river was. I think he said that to save me a dunking!

We proceeded peacefully on the barge to the Sudan until we reached a city whose name I have forgotten. Father did his business, and I did mine. Mother had hired a Thomas Cooke Tour Guide. Going on a Cooke's tour was not my idea of how to see this city. I was with my governess and I said, "We will go on our own. We will get a map and you can read it." The city was rather small, and we barged into all kinds of places.

We both rented bicycles and pedalled away to a nearby village. You never saw the likes of it! The people were all so tall—six feet and some even as much as seven (so they said). I gaped at them and shouted to my governess, "Giants! Giants! Let's look for gold!" She said, "Gold?" in a puzzled voice.

Adults don't understand. So I explained. "When God makes giants it's so they can stand in front of caves which contain hidden treasures. Don't you remember Ali Baba? So let's go look for gold."

Well, it took her about an hour to explain to me that there was no gold hidden anywhere. Even if there was, it would be very dangerous for us to go hunting for it. I said, "Well, that's what we want—danger!" She was too fat (from eating too many Arab sweetmeats) to embrace danger, so I never found out any more about those giants.

We returned to Cairo in an ordinary, comfortable passenger ship, while I dreamt of giants and caverns filled with gold. I even told father and mother about this and said: "Look, if you only had let me follow the giants, we could give the gold to the poor." It took father almost the whole distance to Cairo to straighten me out about this, but secretly I kept my dreams. Even now when I read about how tall the Sudanese are, I remember the giants and the gold and the poor.

This is a bit of an aside, and getting far ahead of my story, but years later in Rome (1951), waiting for an appointment with Cardinal Eugene Tisserant, I met Mother Madeleine, the foundress of the Little Sisters of Jesus. She sat there in her little blue dress, looking like a nursing sister of the Franco-Prussian War, with a little kerchief on her head. She impressed me very much, and she was a very holy person.

I couldn't resist talking to her. She found out that we were part of a lay apostolate and said, "Do you know where our sisters are? In the Sudan." I brightened up like a golden penny. I said, "I'll tell you a story about the Sudan," and proceeded to describe for her the giants and the caves filled with gold! "One of my great childhood dreams," I said, "was to go to the Sudan and open up all those caves and give the gold to all the poor from whom it was probably taken in the first place." (Needless to say, there was no gold, no caves, and no giants standing guard over anything. But there was a truth behind it. The people were slaves, in a manner of speaking. Their golden freedom had been taken away from them—the gold of their dignity had been stolen.)

Mother Madeleine said, "There were a few difficulties for our sisters in the beginning. You know that in certain districts, people do not wear much clothing. They didn't like the idea of people wearing clothes and coming to preach about God. Somehow it didn't fit in with their ideas. I pointed out that our sisters had white skin and would roast in the sun if they didn't wear some protection. The people understood and that solved the problem."

We had a wonderful talk about the apostolate. I said, "I see our approaches are very similar." "Yes," she said, "it seems your ideas are very similar to those of Charles de Foucauld." I was so impressed with her spirit that from then on I just worshiped the Little Sisters and Brothers of Charles de Foucauld. In many buildings of Madonna House we have their special cross (with the Heart of Christ in the middle) as a sign of the spiritual kinship we feel toward them.

During those years we lived in Egypt we often traveled back and forth to Europe or Russia because the heat was so unbearable during the summer. From April on, all the schools were closed. My father turned to ever-dependable Cooke's Agency, and under the paternal supervision of these guides my mother, myself, Serge, our governesses, Serge's English tutor, and our maids, all would be comfortably and safely taken to Europe and then on to Russia.

age 14, with her brother Serge

in her early teens

3. Tombov and My Relatives

Toward the end of our stay in Egypt a most unexpected thing happened to me. I was, you might say, in the first bloom of youth, becoming a little woman. We lived opposite a pasha, a titled Arab, and he came one day to see father. Father didn't speak Arabic, and his translator was in Alexandria (I even remember it was a Sunday). The pasha spoke French, but very poorly. Father sent for me because I spoke Arabic.

The pasha became a bit nervous and said it wasn't quite seemly that I should be the translator in this situation; but since there was no other way, he consented. So I translated. What he started to say was that he wanted to marry me! This pasha had three legitimate wives and I forgot how many concubines.

As I remember, the spiritual leaders of the Arabs are supposed to know how many wives a man has, because the wives and concubines are all entitled to support. Usually a man can have no more than four wives, plus concubines—which surely should be enough for any man!

Anyhow, he wanted to marry me; I would be his fourth wife. According to Egyptian custom, 10 years of age was normal for marriage, and I was about that age.

Father was very wise and "diplomatic" in his response. He said he was honored beyond his wildest dreams that the pasha should desire to marry his daughter. But I was not quite physically developed yet. He also said that I was not ready to be the wife of a pasha because I was not yet intellectually advanced enough to listen to him with the understanding a good wife should have.

29

Two weeks later I was on board a ship with my governess on the way to Paris! I think that was one reason we all left Egypt and returned to Russia. But there were other reasons as well.

Mother was allergic to the intense heat. Also, there were financial problems. Soon after Serge was born, my father had walked into the house and given mother a beautiful diamond necklace. He said, "Mina, my darling, that's my last gift because we are ruined!" Mother said, "Then why did you spend all this money on a diamond necklace?" "Well," he said, "because I wanted to be ruined in style!"

So what could she say except, "It can always be pawned." They both laughed, and then got very serious. They blessed themselves and father said, "God has given, God has taken away. The will of God be done."

I have no recollection of what happened to his job. I was too excited about being ruined! Especially when father had said, "God has given, God has taken away." What was there to worry about?

The next thing I remember is the Rue Chalgrin in Paris. It is one of the little streets close to L'Arche de Triomphe. We had a small apartment there because we were poor now. There was a room for my brother, a room for me, and a room for mother and father. There was a dining room and a kitchen with a coal and gas stove for cooking.

Every morning I accompanied my mother to the markets. Shopping in Paris when you are poor! The haggling is so much fun! You go from stall to stall and gather what you need. Everything was always fresh from the farm and smelled delightful. It's a beautiful memory, the early morning shopping in Paris.

After shopping, and having coffee and croissants with mother, I reluctantly went off to school.

If you want to learn something, you must go to France! I attended the equivalent of high school, where I learned languages, classical literature, history, geography, botany, zoology, and mathematics. I remember that for geography you had to know not only the countries but the little towns as well. You had to take a trip on the Seine (a long river) and name all the cities and towns and villages that you would pass.

30

This school did me a tremendous amount of good because I was sharp and I could learn. But mathematics was another story. I just don't have a mathematical mind. Fortunately the French and the Russians added all your marks and settled for the average. Anyhow, in Paris I learned more in one year than I would have learned in 10 years anywhere else.

Time came when we were no longer ruined! This was a tragedy to my brother and me. One day he went into the bathroom and cried because we were no longer ruined. We loved being ruined. Now there would be no back streets and cheap flats which were so much fun. There would be many servants instead of the one who only came once a day in Paris. In fact, not being ruined turned our whole childish world upside down. It meant not being able to get those lovely warm chestnuts which were sold on the streets of Paris.

My parents then enrolled me in Princess Obolensky High School, a private school run more or less for the nobility. My teachers soon discovered that I could teach French and correct the students' papers. I was able to do the same in German. Consequently, I was allowed to skip all the foreign language courses.

I had a facility for learning that was really amazing. The director of the school called my father in and told him that, notwithstanding my failure in mathematics, I was quite extraordinary, and as far as he was concerned, he would sponsor my enrollment at my early age into the University of Petrograd, to take philosophy or anything else that interested me.

We had an estate in Tombov, south of Russia. As I remember, it consisted of a pretty ancient farmhouse made of logs. You walked into a narrow vestibule and then into a large Russian-style kitchen. At the heart of it stood a huge stove made out of bricks. It had twelve burners of cast iron made by the local blacksmith. It was very efficient. There were also three big ovens and a firebox. One oven could accommodate half a calf! We also cooked on spits over open fires. On top of one oven there was a place to sleep.

There were open shelves on the walls, and all around the shelves were hanging cooking utensils. They were made out of copper, brass, and wood. Wooden dishes were used for leftovers and butter. There were very beautiful platters, artistically painted. Butter was churned in a wooden keg.

I remember a huge table in the corner. In another (eastern) corner, was an icon covered with a bidding towel. (A towel on which the woman of the house embroiders her prayer petitions; she weaves the towel out of flax. Let us say I need hens. I embroider a cock and a hen on the towel and I go to the priest and ask him to bless it so that we have enough money to buy hens and cocks. You could embroider anything—a calf, a baby, a cow, or whatever you wish.)

There were lots of other things in that room. Photographs, a balalaika (musical instrument), things like that. There was a little wooden stairway going upstairs, and I used to walk up that way. The stairs were rather high for me. Strange, I have absolutely no recollection of the upstairs.

On the other hand, I remember the outdoors. The moment you opened the kitchen door you were in a beautiful garden. Not having lawn mowers, we cut the grass with a scythe. Mother hated to have the grass cut, so she cut just a little bit under a tree in the orchard where we could have tea.

I just loved running around that garden. It seemed to me every plant in the world was there. There were daisies and I could say, "He loves me, he loves me not," even if I didn't know whom I was talking about. There were flowers with which to make crowns. A Russian custom was to throw these crowns in the river during the month of May. Then they would cut down a tree and put it into the river. If the crowns came to rest in the tree, the girls who made those crowns would be married that year!

I remember mother collecting mushrooms which were very plentiful in Tombov but this is the extent of my memories of Tombov.

The last I heard about this estate was from Countess Helene Iswolsky whose father had been ambassador to Paris. I had met her in 1937-38 when I went to Paris to write about Catholic Action in Europe. She had become a Catholic, and she was doing a great deal of work among the Russians and others. We lost contact until years later I found out she was in New York. Like many refugees she was reduced by circumstances and landed in America. We eventually became very close friends.

In the 1960s a very rich woman invited the countess to accompany her to Russia. The woman paid for everything, including a trip by car. Helene was allowed to visit many places that were out of bounds for other tourists. As it turned out, she too had had an estate in the Tombov District (we called them *Gooberni* in Russian). Knowing that I also had had some connection with Tombov, she went to the library there and the municipal archives and located our estate. She was very anxious to see it. Upon her return from Russia she brought me the latest information about it. It had become a home for old people.

Helene died in 1975. Before she died I wanted her to contact my brother Serge, who is a real historian, and tell him about her visit, but she never did. She fell ill and died without ever telling too much more about her visit. I have a few letters of hers and they helped refocus some of my memories.

My grandmother was a very interesting person. Her maiden name was Vernet, and her father was a painter of horses. Three of his paintings hang in the Louvre. I always called her "Grandmother." I never knew her first name, and I don't to this day. I have a picture of her with my uncle, Constantine.

As I remember her in my childhood, she had an abundance of gray hair like my mother's. Grandmother's only reached below her waist, while mother's fell almost to her ankles. Grandmother's hair was very fine and silky, and I delighted in brushing it. I invented a thousand hairdos for her, and she always patiently endured everything.

There was about her a strange world of tradition. Her family had been refugees from France and its political upheavals.

I spent enchanting years with her in Russia, when I was about six to nine years old. I remember that she had brought from France a lot of dainty little boxes. They were ornamental, finely made, and inlaid with beautiful mother-of-pearl. Grandmother used to say, "These are very precious to me. I brought them with me instead of dolls." I could understand how she could cherish them. They were fantastic. Whenever I went to see her I would spend half of my time poking around those boxes. Inside I found all kinds of interesting things. In one box, a beautifully inlaid crucifix. In another, a medallion. Then, you pressed a secret button and presto! another drawer would open. It had a picture of a man all in ruffles and a high collar. Someone from the 17th century or thereabouts. My grandmother looked at it and said, "Ah, this is one of your ancestors, Mr. So-and-So." Then she would tell me the story of his chateau.

"Did he really have a chateau?" I asked. "Yes," my grandmother responded, "the Vernets had a chateau. But you have to remember, there are chateaus and there are chateaus. Some people, like the king, had king-size chateaus. Ours wasn't like that. Think of a little chateau hidden amongst the vinelands of the Rhone Valley."

I had never visited there, but my mother also told me about it. Grandmother described the furniture, and how the people worked in the vineyards and crushed the grapes with their bare feet. How clean their feet had to be for that!

I certainly felt at times as if I were French. I don't remember where I learned French. The origins of my speaking French (and German and Russian for that matter) are lost to memory, because I don't remember studying them. The governesses spoke these languages, and I just talked with them. My grandmother spoke French and oh how she would roll the r's! I used to say, "Grandmother, why don't you go back to France?" She answered, "I don't want to go back to France, because I'm Russian." "But," I said, "your married name is Thompson." It always puzzled me that two names like Vernet and Thompson added up to being a Russian!

You remember that at one point I left home to go and live with my grandmother because I was angry with my mother. Grandmother never gave me cookies or anything like they do in America. She would tell me stories, endless and interesting stories about France. Then she would get out all those little boxes and it seemed that stories popped out of every drawer. Everything she said was very interesting, and I listened, absolutely enthralled.

My Aunt Jania, which would be "Genevieve" in English, became Catholic. Everybody was against it except grandmother. So I said, "Grandmother, why aren't you against all this?"

"Oh," she said, "our family is Catholic." It dawned on me when I grew up that, of course, the Vernets would all be Catholics, because they were French. She added: "We all became Orthodox when we came to Russia. It's the same thing."

Jania always had a rosary hanging over her bed. She used to talk to me and tell me French fairy tales—*Les Contes de Fee*. She always called me "Katinka," never Katia or Catherine. She was a very wonderful person.

How my grandmother married my grandfather is a complete mystery to me. She told me many times, but I wasn't interested; I was interested in her. Grandfather had died before I was born so I never met him and consequently he didn't mean too much to me.

Grandmother would often talk to me about being a woman, and this is how she would begin: "Katinka, you are a woman now."

"Yes," I answered, "it's different from being a man. The boys are different from the girls."

"That isn't important at the moment," she would say. "What is important is that you acquire womanly virtues."

One night I had realized that grandmother considered me a tomboy, so that's why she spoke of "womanly virtues." I must say, she had a point. I was a tomboy when I come to think of it. I was brought up with my brother Serge (who was about seven years younger than I) and his chums.

For example, Serge and I used to ski together. He was small, had smaller skis, and so he could easily ski around the tree stumps which dotted the hilly field near our home. One day he dared me to do the same, and I succumbed to his dare. I skied around those stumps right down to the bottom of the field, where I ran into my father! He was a little pale. "You're old enough to know better," he said. I explained that Serge had dared me to do it. Father was a little mad at Serge and told him to be a brother and protector to me. Father made it clear to me that I was stupid to act on a dare from him.

I haven't mentioned yet that my father had a son, Vsevolod, by his first wife, Catherine, who died giving birth to him. Consequently, he was my half-brother. When I was 12, he was 21 or so, and I didn't see very much of him. While we traveled around, he stayed in Russia; when we were in Russia together, we got along fine.

But back to grandmother. She had deep blue eyes, gray hair, and an aquiline nose. She was rather thin, and followed the horrible custom in those days of wearing a corset that pushed her bust up! I used to say, "Grandmother, my God, why do you wear that horrible thing?" because I thought it was the most awful contraption imaginable. (But she did look lovely in it!)

Grandmother could tell fairy tales at the drop of a hat. I think she made up every one, and they always had to do with courts and rich people and princes and princesses. One story in particular I remember very well.

There was a beautiful princess who slept in a turret. She had to walk upstairs every night and her mother would lock the door behind her so that no harm would come to her. There was a very handsome prince who wanted to marry her, but her parents had decided that she was too young. They locked her up in the turret every night so that she wouldn't elope.

In grandmother's story, the turret was as high as the sky. The prince got his people to construct a silken ladder as long as the turret was high. But how to get it into the hands of the princess? That was the question.

Well, for many years the princess had been feeding this bird, a very beautiful bird. It was the size of a crane or an eagle. Each day the prince tied a section of the ladder to the bird's foot as it flew up to eat the crumbs the princess left out for it. So, every morning, she unrolled a part of the silken ladder. It was so cunningly arranged that all she had to do was to fit the parts together. (Even she could do that!) Finally, the last part arrived. It came with a letter telling her that the prince would be waiting at the bottom that very night with his servants and a horse for her.

It was a moonlit night, but nobody was guarding the turret. Who could possibly get up there! The princess put the ladder on two hooks fixed to the turret wall, and started to descend. Oh, it was dangerous! (And grandmother could really make it sound so. I used to sit there and almost stop breathing!) Finally, she made it down. There was a saddled horse for her. She jumped on the horse and they galloped away.

The church they were headed for was about 15 kilometers away. But shortly before they arrived, the church had been besieged by brigands and the priest killed and everything stolen. The next church was very, very far away. They decided to rest awhile, then continue on their way.

Do you know what happened? They never reached their goal. They got lost in the forest. Then grandmother would say in hushed and dramatic tones, "That's why any time you go into the forest at

36

night you will hear the hoofbeats of horses. They are the horses of the prince and the princess." The moral of the story: "True love is a very beautiful thing and it will always find a way."

The story had a special meaning for I knew all about eloping. Father had often told us the story of how Count Usoopoff had eloped. This count was the father of the man who killed Rasputin and was a friend of my father's. Father had been the best man at his wedding. The count's bride-to-be had descended from her home on a silk ladder just like in the fairy tales, then had rushed away in a sleigh to get married. It was all very exciting.

Yes, my grandmother seems alive to me; so do the little boxes of French treasures, the fairy tales, her big smile and her patting me on the head saying, "Katinka, you should learn womanly virtues because you are a woman. I think you will go very far."

My mother and father met in a rather romantic circumstance. My mother was a good seamstress and favored what today are called caftan-style dresses. One day she went out to a hill to gather wild lilies of the valley. Suddenly the rains came, a real storm, drenching her. So there she was, you might say practically naked, because the ordinary white material of her caftan just clung to her body.

My father was hunting below the hill when he saw her and was evidently fascinated by this beautiful woman, her hair falling down to her ankles and her clothes plastered to her like a statue. They were married within three months!

I don't know if my mother's father or her grandfather was of the nobility. I know that my mother went to the Smolensky Institute which catered especially to children of the nobility. During high school, which takes a long time in Russia, she specialized in music and graduated as a concert pianist.

Father was a hunter, as I mentioned. All children think of their father as a great hunter, but mine really was! Once a year he went hunting grizzly bears, which in those days was not a simple matter. Mother used to light all the vigil lights in front of the icons for his protection. You could only kill one bear (and who needed more than one!).

When the hunter found his grizzly he had to face him with nothing more than a long, stiletto-like lance. As the grizzly stood on his hind legs, towering over the hunter, there were only a few seconds in which to plunge the lance into the grizzly's heart. The hunter didn't get a second chance! Every year father returned with a grizzly, and without a scratch on him. So I felt that he was a great hunter.

Why kill bears? For food. For their warm pelts. We didn't put them on the floor as is the custom in America. The pelt was used as a coverlet on those long winter sleigh rides. So father hunted, but only for what he needed.

At that time there were no special hunting laws in the forests of Russia, but people respected the laws of nature. Of course, sometimes people forgot they were Christians (especially in those organized hunts from the cities) and hunted indiscriminately. But generally speaking, people only hunted for what they needed. It was mostly a matter of food. They hunted fowl, bears, deer and other animals, but everybody understood that you could kill too many and endanger the species. It was a sensitivity very much like that of the American Indians who kept the laws of nature and did not abuse what God had given them.

My parents, and all my ancestors, were gentlemen farmers. Even the noblest of the noble had a farm, and these farms were run by superintendents.

There were only a few occupations in Russian society. You either were a farmer yourself, or a gentleman farmer, or you joined the armed forces. You could be a bureaucrat, belonging to a sort of Russian pentagon, and work there all your life. You might also be involved in the life at court and attend all the social and diplomatic functions.

Russia had its feudal system, something like the England of old. First came the peasants. Interestingly enough, the Russian word for "peasant" is *kristian*, and usually he was a tenant farmer, although he might own some land of his own.

Next came the three divisions of what was known as the "merchant class." There were the small shopkeepers, owners of small grocery stores and the like. Then there were the owners of the bigger shops as on Nevsky Street in St. Petersburg. Finally came the proprietors of the largest stores—not as big as Sears and T. Eaton Co., but they were quite large.

The priests had a separate status. Usually they chose their wives from other priestly families. This was no problem since priests usually had many children. As you know, they married before they were ordained.

Next came the nobility. From the lowest to the highest there were seven degrees, and they were called *Bojari*. The merchant trade and the nobility were not supposed to mingle. My aunt's husband once was snubbed by the Tsar because he noticed some flour on his shoulder and said, "We noticed some flour here." A nobleman could grow the grains to be milled, but it was not proper to mill them himself.

I know that I have not paid too much attention to dates and geography as I have told this story, but it is my early experience of Russia and my childhood, as I remember it and as I wish to relate it.

1925, a portrait

4. Education to Womanhood

Mother was an extraordinary person. She believed that you shouldn't ask a domestic to do any kind of work that you hadn't been trained to do yourself, and so she was really a quite well-rounded person. Now it was my turn to be educated according to mother's ideas!

We had quite a large household. There were about 14 servants, a very good "cordon bleu" cook, assisted by a "vegetable girl," as we used to call her, and a kitchen maid who attended to the eternal cleaning and polishing. There was a laundry and a laundress to preside over it. If you think a Russian laundry of my time was just a matter of throwing clothes in a washer, then in a dryer, and pressing them with an electric iron, you are gravely mistaken!

First and foremost, we didn't even have a scrub board. Everything was done by hand, and it had to be as white as Snow White herself! The laundress began by soaking all the white clothes in cold water. If they weren't clean enough, back into the soaking they went. Then they were boiled. You can see some of the boilers in the museums. You stirred while the clothes were boiling, having added some homemade soap. Then came the rinsing in hot water, the bluing, and the hanging on the line outside. In the winter, the larger sheets were often laid out on the snow where the sun and snow whitened them.

Next came the ironing. We had a cast iron stove. The irons were slightly tilted so they wouldn't get too hot. If the garments burned, you had to start all over again beginning with the soaking! As the irons cooled off you had to keep changing them, and this was no easy work.

41

I took my turn in the kitchen. Please, young people, don't visualize being a vegetable girl in a Russian kitchen as simply a matter of scraping and cutting carrots. Oh no! You had to make flowers out of them! Here your imagination could run wild. The same with the turnips and kohlrabi and other vegetables. Even asparagus was braided gently and served in a special sauce. Other vegetables such as cabbage, turnips, and peppers were stuffed with special fillings.

The vegetable girl learned all these arts under the eagle eye of an expert cook who rejected anything that wasn't perfect. I shed many a tear over my imperfections!

Russians cooked in brass and copper pots so as not to poison the food. Even the copper pots had to be lined with a special material before you could use them. The outside, the copper itself, had to be polished after every meal.

The ingredients for polishing were as follows: first, elbow grease and plenty of it; second, black bread soured especially for this purpose, or rye flour, also soured. You slapped this stuff all over the copper, and when it dried you washed it off and began polishing. You polished and polished and polished! The cook was quite lavish in the use of pots and pans, so you had a lot of polishing to do. But I must admit that seeing the shining pots hanging on the kitchen walls was worth all the effort. It was a really beautiful sight.

The washing up was done by the waitress and the housemaid, and the silver polishing by us—the kitchen maid and the vegetable girls. We didn't have Silvo or Brasso. We just had the good old rye bread or rye flour, although later on there was a powder that helped. Nonetheless, it was a real chore after serving a meal for 50 people.

When my time in the kitchen ended I was transferred to the laundry; when I finished there I became the housemaid. In this job I could work a bit faster because I was quick and healthy. Mother wouldn't allow me to wait on strangers, only the family. My waiting on the family was often punctuated by such helpful, joking remarks as, "Don't get the gravy down my neck"; "Hold it straight"; "Follow the butler and don't go ahead of him"; "Don't rush people."

Finally I was put into the sewing room, which was really a

mending room. Girls, if you want to see a well-mended sock, where the mend is practically invisible, I can demonstrate for you. It cost me many a tear to learn, and many of them fell onto the socks! Patching bedding of all kinds, patching clothes—this became second nature to me on my treadle machine. There were also weaving, spinning, and embroidery—hobbies I chose for myself. I also learned bookbinding, and eventually graduated to metal-etching.

All these things happened mostly during my long summer vacations, for during the rest of the year I had to study. All through my childhood and early youth I was indoctrinated in the fact that the duty of the moment was the duty of God. When I was fairly little, I thought that God was right by my side, embroidering, etc. I didn't have to make too many decisions about what to do with my time, since the duty of the moment came from authority.

Speaking of authority, I was an obedient child although mischievous. I had lots of fun and could tell many stories about the fun I had. I studied music and played the piano, but my favorite hobby was reading.

I am often amazed at people who say they have no time for reading. I used to hide under the sofa, escaping from my governess for a few moments, to read a few paragraphs from a favorite book. I read every time I went to the bathroom. Besides, there was lots of free time when I could read, and I was encouraged to do so. Wherever we went to live, whether for a long or short interval, the first thing I saw the carpenters do was make shelves for the books my parents cherished. Even as a small child, I was given those linen books you couldn't tear. Down through the years I have always had shelves for my favorite books.

As regards health, I certainly was never pampered. Disease was taken in stride, and so was pain.

I remember when I was a little girl of about seven, I was walking along the Mediterranean beach with my father. I fell and slashed my knee on a stone and started to yell like a banshee. My father dipped my knee into the saltwater of the sea and I yelled some more. He said to me, "You don't like Jesus Christ very much, do you? He was crucified for you and endured a lot of pain. You just have a little scratch and you yell like nobody's business. If you can't bear physical pain, child, how will you bear the pain of the heart and of the mind that will certainly come to you?" I didn't understand what he said at the time, but I understand it now. At no time, then, was I allowed to make a big deal out of pain, which was often related to the pains of Jesus Christ.

Sickness was treated according to its severity. Ordinary colds were a matter of staying in bed and drinking liquids. In more serious situations, doctors were called in and absolute obedience to their orders was required.

Normally I slept on a very hard bed with a small mattress, thin blankets, and an open window. The first thing in the morning was a cold shower and a rub with a huge towel. In the winter, mother believed in washing the face with snow. She said it was good for the complexion. We had a sauna in our home. Right after the sauna my mother threw me into the snow, or I was dipped into an ice-cold pond. It was really wonderful to be rubbed afterwards with a big, heavy, warm towel.

My mother was born with a green thumb; in fact, she had 10 of them! Anything she touched, grew. There is a story about the holy monks which I often think of in connection with my mother's green thumb.

There was a very holy monk living in the desert in a little hut. A young monk heard about him and came to talk with him. The young monk wanted to imitate the holy life of the solitary. The old monk told him how to pray, and especially how to be silent. Then he said: "See that stick there?" (Sticks in the desert are really dry.) "Water it three times a day. When it puts forth green shoots, then you will be holy."

When the young monk reached the age of 90 or so, the stick finally bloomed. I often think that if the old monk had told my mother to put the stick in the ground and water it, it would have blossomed in two days!

In Finland we had a beautiful half-acre garden with all kinds of flowers. The tragedy was that it had to be watered by hand! Even in the lovely Russian and Finnish summers, we had dry spells. We filled pails with water, then poured the water into sprinkling cans. Half an acre! It was back-breaking work. Mother said it was good for the muscles. My brother helped with his little pails until he was big enough to do the job, too.

Another half-acre was in strawberries, raspberries, and

other small berries. We also had nut trees. Thanks be to God, some of the nuts grew without water, or I would have gone nuts myself!

We also had a vegetable garden. I learned how to look after vegetables from the hoeing and preparation, to the planting and harvesting. Different vegetables need different preparation. The French have what they call "haricots," namely, green beans, kohlrabi, peas, tomatoes and the like. Mother's idea was that I had to know all these things, otherwise I would not be competent to run an estate and be a gentleman farmer's wife. She was most exacting! I learned all the fine arts of being a woman, and I learned them with a certain amount of discipline because periodically I would rebel!

I was also introduced to beekeeping. Hives were made out of straw. You couldn't, of course, order your bees from somebody. We used to go early in the spring ourselves and acquire swarms out of the trees, gathering colonies with a big net. Once you captured the queen, the rest of the hive followed. Then we stuck them in our little straw hives. The colony then began to construct its own honeycombs. I watched it all and was quite fascinated. Mother had me read books on the subject so that I knew and understood what was happening. In the winter, the bees either left their hives, or we placed them in the cellar.

Then there was the milking. At one time we had a herd of 80 or 90 cows. We sold fresh, unsalted butter which was very much in demand. I still remember the man who came to fetch the butter. He and I used to chat and he always had a lot to tell about the neighbors.

We also had two or three shepherds to go out to pasture with the cows.

Mother taught me how to milk, being a very good milker herself. We didn't have machines, of course, and it was a very interesting process. If cold, we milked in the stable, and when it was warmer, outside. We arrived on the scene with a stool tied around the waist. Our hands were often busy, so it was a way of always having the stool with you. I would sit down beside the cow, place the pail underneath and splash a few shots of milk into the pail to wash it out. It was already clean, but this was just to make it superclean. I threw the milk on the ground. It wasn't wasted:

the dogs and chickens lapped it up. Then I would begin to milk seriously.

We didn't have cream separators in those days, but we had a very, very long underground cellar, like a root cellar. It was very well constructed, with two or three rows of shelves for the milk pails. The roof was made of wood, with a thick covering of sod, so that the cellar was nice and cool all the time.

Mother had quite a few "milkmaids" as they were called. Their job, and mine as well, was to go around with a very flat ladle (made of zinc or some other metal) and skim the cream into a pail. When this was done, we brought the cream to the buttery where the wooden churns were. The maids pushed a wooden plunger up and down inside the churn and eventually butter formed.

There was another type of churn, highly prized. It consisted of a huge wooden barrel with a handle at the end to turn it. Thus you turned the barrel and in this way the butter was made much faster.

Actually, if large quantities aren't needed, all that is required to make butter is to put some cream in a sealed jar and shake it for three-quarters of an hour or so. It's very simple, but hard! Our way too was hard. At the end of making, say, a hundred pounds of butter, you could barely lift your arms!

Still, I didn't mind it. And later in life I was sad to see us acquire milking machines at Madonna House. Somehow a machine and cow just don't go together. The gentle fingers of the person should touch the gentle teats of the cow. It's such a natural combination of beauty. This is how the cow gives milk to the calf. We don't pump milk by machine out of a woman's breast for her child. I guess I'm just nostalgic these days. Pretty soon there won't be any cows and we'll just have a machine that makes milk! That's how I feel sometimes.

As I try to explain these first 15 or so years of my life, my mind goes back somewhat unwillingly. It was such a beautiful time, and I have so many lovely memories. These conflict quite a bit with what is happening now in the world. For me personally, my childhood is a place where I can hide in a world that was normal, a world where nature and man were in harmony, a world where man took from nature only what God wanted him to take.

But to continue on with my education to womanhood!

My mother was always suggesting that I take up some form of handicraft. Thus I learned embroidery, since this was particularly the thing to do when you were a little girl. I learned bookbinding, and we have here at Madonna House a book that I bound when I was a little girl. I learned knitting and crocheting and some weaving. The weaving was a very simple kind: the remnants of our dresses were cut up and made into rugs.

People in the area helped mother make linen. It was really fine material, especially when it was made with flax directly from our own fields. You appreciated it also, since you had to beat and beat the flax until only the fibers were left. Nor was it easy to straighten out the fibers with only your hands. But our women managed, as did everybody else. Many a fine linen was woven in our weaving quarters, which was a large, long room with all kinds of weaving equipment. It was lovely to go there in the evenings. Yes, those were the days!

So varied was my life at home that it is difficult to write it all down. It was such a happy period of my life. Occasionally I was left in some school for a month or so when father was traveling. This happened in Montreux, Switzerland, when my parents went off together someplace. I remember Lake Geneva, and I remember that the school specialized in foreign students like myself. We often went on trips to learn about the country, but a month is a short time.

I attended several schools in different countries. Far from upsetting me as changes in schools are supposed to do, I made friends easily and through these travels and schools learned many languages. There was a time when I spoke modern Greek, Russian, French, English, German, Arabic, and understood Serbian, Bulgarian, and Polish. My parents constantly aided and encouraged this wide approach to the world. Father would take out maps and show me where we were, and tell me legends and stories about the people among whom we were living or about to live. This gave me a very broad education to say the least.

I was, therefore, exposed to various races, foods, and lifestyles vastly different from those I knew in Russia. And my parents were wonderful tutors. They always told me to eat everything that was put on my plate, to "do as the Romans do," that was, to be polite and not say, "But in Russia we do it thus and so."

Yes, it was a wonderful time of my life. People were in love with spiritual as well as material creation. I don't think many understand this about the Russian people. The key to the Russian character is this: The whole heart, the whole person is, in a way, God-centered. Some are evil-centered, but they always seem to have one hand in the holy water!

It is said that Stalin went to confession before he died. Almost like Goethe, Lenin cried out, "What if there is a God!"

Helen Iswolsky told me of Stalin's deathbed confession. She heard it from the nanny of Stalin's daughter, Svetlana. This nanny, in the middle of the night, opened the door to a monk, and Stalin confessed his sins before he died. She said that the next day this monk was shot by Stalin's assistants. It can be verified by Stalin's daughter, and probably will be someday. As Churchill said, the Russians are a mystery wrapped in an enigma! That's why politics with Russia is very hazardous for pragmatic Americans.

But I digress. I have arrived now to the time of my first marriage.

5. My Marriage and the War

My father had three sisters, Virginia, Vera, and Olga. Vera was a governess in a de Hueck family, and the oldest son fell in love with her and married her. My husband, Boris, was born from their union. He was, then, my first cousin. Baron Boris de Hueck came from a Dutch-German family, and how he became (or his ancestors became) part of the nobility is very interesting. One of the family had distinguished himself in battle, and Peter the Great greeted him afterwards, extending his hand and saying, "Congratulations, *Baron* de Hueck." That's how his family entered the nobility.

I was 15 and a half years old when I was married. I was married to the Baron in St. Petersburg on January 25. As usual, I'm not too sure of the year. According to some remaining records, it was 1912, but the date I remember is 1915.

Boris was Orthodox, so we were married in an Orthodox church. There were difficulties due to the fact that we were first cousins. One of the daughters of the Tsar had fallen in love with her first cousin. Ruling families were so interrelated that the Tsar forbade this marriage and all marriages between first cousins. Special permission had to be obtained for my marriage, which my father arranged. My marriage in the Orthodox church was recognized as valid by the Catholic church.

It was a tremendous wedding, with 300 guests attending. My trousseau was fine linen and real lace, all handmade by the nuns. I wore a dress imported from France. You should have seen me in all this finery! Years later I gave my wedding veil to my son's wife. Four page boys were needed to carry my train.

49

On returning from church after a wedding there was the custom of everyone drinking champagne and then breaking their glasses by throwing them into a big basket in front of the fireplace. Well, everyone drank, and everyone broke their glasses! I circulated among the guests and tried to attend to everything as befits a new bride. Then I dressed for travel.

I wore a very beautiful blue moire dress and blouse, made out of soft China silk, with a little blue beret. That was my going-away outfit. My husband's wedding present to me consisted of a necklace of beautifully matched pearls and earrings. (Everyone said I was unlucky to receive pearls, which they connected with tears.) They were his family's pearls, precious heirlooms. I also received all the jewelry of the de Huecks that accrued to the eldest son.

Then we left for Riga. I have a few pictures taken at that time. Riga was the seat of the de Hueck family because Peter the Great had settled the first de Hueck there. Riga had a de Hueck Street, and the de Hueck ancestral home was located there. This house was actually a series of medieval houses connected one to the other. Inside were corridors and corridors of de Hueck portraits. Boris and I were supposed to be painted, the last pair, but due to the war it never happened.

Russians rarely went on honeymoons, nor did we have the custom of the husband picking you up and carrying you across the threshold. We just walked into our new house and knelt before the icon of our Lady, and prayed. Then, after the marriage act, we again knelt before the icon of our Lady and asked her to make our marriage fruitful and happy. That was the custom for the wedding night.

Then, life would continue. The husband would attend to his farming, or whatever other work he had to do. Maybe he took a week or so off, but that was about all. Sometimes, of course, the very rich would go on a "honeymoon." They had words for it—*Medovi Mesits* "honey" and "moon"—but it doesn't exactly mean what it means in the West.

Boris was studying in Riga to be an architect and graduated within a year. I remember helping him with the history of art. The examiner would say: "I would like you to draw the profile of a column of an Aztec temple." Then the student had to make all the designs and drawings. For his final examination he presented a scale model and plans for an amphitheatre such as they had in Greece. It was very beautiful and he received first or second prize. He graduated from Russia's best university. (I remember he got 90 per cent on the final exam!)

In Russia, an architect also had to be a civil engineer. So Boris also had to present a project for his engineering examination. He drew up an intricate railway system to be built in Siberia. Thus he graduated both as a civil engineer and an architect. On the side, because he was absolutely crazy about mathematics (he lived, in a sense, by mathematics), he studied astronomy. He was endlessly computing the distances between the stars and things like that.

He was an artist as well, and was always sketching and painting; I still have some of his sketchbooks. He loved to draw people, and would sit and sketch pictures of sailors, prostitutes, poor women, rich women, and so on.

By the time he finished his studies, the war had already begun and he enlisted. Because he had been a cadet and had graduated from a military college, he was eligible to be an officer. He joined the *Sapeurs*, that is, the Engineering Corps.

In the meantime, I studied Red Cross nursing. The Russians had mobilized an army of 20 million soldiers, but they had few nurses, so I offered my services. Red Cross nursing in those days provided a very good training. They really prepared you for duty at the front where I was sent upon graduating.

I was appointed to the First Army, and so was the Baron. We seldom saw each other because we were busy at different occupations. Very soon (because I had a loud voice and was a good organizer) they put me in charge of the "soup kitchen." My job was to see to it that the soldiers had their proper meals—fish chowder on Fridays, and meat soups on other days.

Visualize the scene. The kitchen was behind the trenches. At mealtime we moved with a huge, horse-drawn cauldron from trench to trench, dispensing food. Soldiers were allowed two pounds of rye bread for each meal. This was the job of me and my assistants—cutting, weighing, cutting, weighing—all day long. The people assigned as cooks really knew how to cook. Most of them were overage and so were not engaged in the fighting. But

51

they could fight if necessary. I had, I think, eight cooks under me. Quite an army in itself, and it was quite a strenuous job to supervise everything.

At the stove (which was on wheels) we burned only wood and everything was boiled. Soup might be cooking on one stove, and beans on another. Or even stew on a third. But every day there would certainly be soup and pounds of black bread. Plus tea, endless rounds of tea.

The Russian army was divided into groups of 10 men, and a foreman was appointed for the week. It was his job to get the food for his men with big pails, then return to his group and distribute it. His helper carried the bread. Mealtime was very busy!

Besides the supervision of the kitchen, I had to keep an eye on the little First Aid centers that dotted the fields in back of the trenches. At any moment I might be called to lend a hand there. On one occasion I worked 60 hours without sleep.

Roads were very poor. We cut down trees and laid them out one next to the other, corduroy style. The sick were put into covered wagons and, drawn by two horses, taken over this very rough road to the rear. It was terrible, but Russians are strong and they survived.

Usually, near the hospital, a tent served as a "welcome area" where books, chess games, cards and so forth were available. We could relax there by helping to cheer people up. New arrivals spent their first night there. There was also a piano and we all sang our beloved Russian songs. The next morning, at four or five o'clock, the soldiers would leave again for the front. I used to get a little depressed watching those young men leave in good shape, but knowing that in a few days they would be dead, or have an arm or leg missing.

So I was in charge of the kitchen and the recreation area, and the doctor was in charge of the hospital and Red Cross stations.

One night, while I was sleeping, the field telephone rang. The doctor in charge was calling and said, "Catherine, your horse is saddled and ready. You've got to go and check the 'peninsula.' " This was a promontory between the Russian and German lines. He said, "You've got to go to the peninsula because fighting has broken out there and it's really terrible. In the second or third

52

trench there is no nurse. You are the closest one now and better than any graduate nurse. Go!"

So I went, and it was quite a trip. About 10 miles. When I got to this promontory bullets were buzzing all around. I miraculously escaped unharmed. It was doubly miraculous because on the ride my horse had stumbled and I fell off. There's nothing to falling off a horse, but he got nervous, and at the sight of my white veil kicked me in the back with his left foot. He was so sorry afterwards that he licked my face and helped to revive me. When I came to I remembered what I had to do.

The problem was getting back on the horse. That took some courage. I coughed up blood every time I tried to climb into the stirrup. Finally I made it. "The duty of the moment is the duty of God," I said to myself. Only God knows how I made the last two miles, because every time I moved I spat blood.

I arrived and found that there were no doctors and no nurses. I forgot about my injury and proceeded to nurse the wounded to the best of my ability. In the middle of it all the doctor arrived.

He took one look at the wounded, and one look at me, and he said, "You've got to go to the hospital!" I really was spitting blood badly. This was one of the reasons I received a decoration for bravery. There were others, but this was one of them. I never thought much about it, for I was only doing my duty.

On another occasion during my service at the front, I came to the doctor and said, "All we have is about a hundred or so pounds of meat, but it's all full of maggots. What am I supposed to do?" He said, "Do we have any vinegar?" We found a huge vat, and soaked the meat in the vinegar. Within 24 hours all the maggots rose to the surface because they couldn't stand the vinegar. They floated on the top and the cook removed them with a ladle. We washed the meat with cold water, then warm water, then made soup out of it. And that's what we ate! That was among the first stirrings in the front lines that something had gone wrong with the food deliveries.

Very soon after that the front collapsed. Kerenski allowed the political parties to campaign. I heard the communists talk, and they had a good sales pitch. They simply said to the soldiers, "Why don't you go back to your villages, seize the estates of the landlords, and divide them amongst yourselves!" That was the one thing the Russian peasant always wanted more of: land. So they left the front, took the train, and went home.

It was a very tragic situation. The hospital simply dissolved. The wounded were carried away on stretchers, and those less seriously injured hobbled away on crutches. Soldiers would argue with train engineers on the platforms. One said, "You will go north. I want to go to Moscow or Petrograd." Another said, "I want to go south." The engineer was really in a quandary. Finally, the soldiers decided to draw lots. It was north. That suited me fine, because I wanted to go to Petrograd where Boris and I had our home, and where I hoped my father would be. I only witnessed one of these scenes, but that kind of thing went on all the time in the confusion.

It was some ride! Normally, the trip would only have taken 11 hours at the maximum. It took us almost six days. At each station the scene of "north or south" was repeated again, and we shuffled back and forth. The train was completely filled. If you wanted to go to the bathroom, you just went—because the door was always open! Nobody paid any attention. You also slept on top of one another in the corridors. It was horrible.

At one point we came to a small station and the engine balked. Something went wrong. The engineer announced, "You'll have to sleep here until we fix it." I remember sleeping on a table and somebody pushing me off. Then I slept on the floor. There was nothing to eat, but we did have water.

When I finally arrived in Petrograd I had lost quite a bit of weight. I was also still in considerable pain from the injury I suffered when kicked by the horse. Mother was safe in Finland, staying near the big river, Imatral, close to our estate there. I found my father and asked him for some food, and he gave me some tea and bread. It was an extraordinary treat at the time to have tea and bread. There was no sugar or anything else. When you are beginning to starve, after a period of terrible desire, hunger stops. That's a dangerous time.

Fortunately, Boris and I were reunited. He arrived a couple days after I did, not knowing that I was there. I didn't know he was in the city either. We went to our apartment on Geslerovsky Street which was very luxurious and very beautiful. But it didn't stay that way for long! Boris, who never was very robust, was pretty weak already.

Our beautiful piano was still there. Boris and I both played, and sang very well. I loved violets, and we always used to have violets on the piano. We had placed an order with the florists to renew them every week, as well as the roses and other flowers. The last violets were still there, quite dried out. The icons were there also, and in Boris' den stood a regal desk and beautiful chairs covered with real leather. We walked around in all this beauty, but there was nothing to eat!

Then we began our search for food. We were called "bourgeois" and "aristocrats." We were not given any ration stamps, so we couldn't buy anything. Boris got sick because he had been shell-shocked and gassed during the war. While he stayed in bed, I took a clean pail and went to the homes of the communists. I knew where they lived. I went to the back alleys and looked through the garbage cans of the communists. They were the only ones who had any garbage. If the cans were empty, I knew they were people like us.

One day, I remember, I found 10 leaves of cabbage. It was really something to have 10 leaves of cabbage! Praying for a little more, I went on my way. I found six boiled potatoes that somebody had thrown out. They were already slightly moldy, but I took them just the same. From somewhere else I obtained dried apricots, just a few. I brought these treasures home, washed them, and mixed everything together. I heated the potatoes and the cabbage and made two little bowls of soup out of them.

Each day I began getting dizzier and dizzier as I went on my food rounds. At night I took a little flashlight with me. There were lots of people in the streets, but because I was poorly clad nobody could tell who I was.

One day, with a babushka on my head, I was making my rounds with my little pail. Walking ahead of me was a woman enveloped in a rich Karakul (black Persian lamb) coat. Three soldiers came along and one of them exclaimed, "Ah, look, aristocrat, bourgeois!" He pulled out his revolver and shot the woman dead. He turned and said to me, "Little girl, why don't you take her coat? You will be warm. You have nothing to wear." "I can't, I can't," I shouted, and ran away.

Yes, I walked for food among the dead bodies to sustain life. I vividly recall the stench, for Petrograd was like a cemetery of open graves. The dead were left lying there, where they fell. Sometimes you had to step over them, and they smelled terrible!

We passed quite a few months in this condition. With my little pail, I walked miles and miles for food. Then I couldn't walk anymore; I was too weak. Now there was no piano left in our apartment, nor anything else. The communists had taken everything away from us. We were now sleeping on the floor, covering ourselves with such things as we could find. We decided to go to Finland while we were still able to physically navigate.

We left for Finland and arrived at some friends who lived near the border. "We cannot keep you in our house," they said, "the communist patrol comes by several times a day. But you can hide in the pigsty." We hid there with swine all around, and the patrol passed by without seeing us.

We got out. Actually, we had only a few steps to go to reach the gully which separated Russia from Finland. We went down into the gully and were spotted by the patrol. Shooting started. We were very weak, but we held each other up and ran.

At the bottom of the gully was a little rivulet, like a brook. We quickly washed ourselves off as best we could, then started climbing the Finnish side of the gully. The bullets were still coming, but it was twilight and they couldn't see us too clearly. There were bushes also.

Finally we made it! Some Finns were waiting for us, and they were very nice to us. They put us into a sauna, gave us some food and clothing. We really couldn't eat very much right then because we were too exhausted and excited over our escape.

We were planning to make our way to the village near our estate, Kiskila, but they warned us that that village had become communist. But we had no choice, so we went to Kiskila. This estate, a villa facing a beautiful fjord, was a wedding gift from my husband; he had built it himself. There were many acres, and it was in my favorite forest. We had called the estate, "Merri-Lokki," meaning "Sea Gull," because it was perched high up on the rocks.

The villagers came out to meet us—and they were all communists! They decreed that we should die by starvation. They had

56

taken all the food out of the villa before our arrival. They left us wood to keep warm, so that our sufferings might be prolonged. However, they had overlooked a lot of potatoes which were frozen under some straw. We were able to bake potatoes at night and eat them.

But slowly, slowly, I lost weight. Slowly my arms became bloated, like in dropsy; so did my face. Strange, red blotches appeared, and I looked funny, with my puffed-out face, yet thin. I shrank slowly. My hair fell out—all of it—in pieces the size of silver dollars. My head was covered with tufts of remaining hair and bald spots. I had had beautiful hair which reached to the middle of my back.

Then my teeth began to loosen. I didn't have a single filling, but they began to loosen. I went into some kind of coma; still, I was aware of everything that was happening. There were two canaries in the house with us. They were using my hair to make a nest. A dog wandered in with a bone, and Boris and I fought over it! The dog ran away.

Most of the time we just lay on the bed. I was in a state of suspended animation. I was constantly dreaming of food. Strangely enough, I didn't dream of meat but of *vatroschka*, which is a cottage cheese pie. I dreamt of pancakes with this cottage cheese. I dreamt of *pelmeni* filled with vegetables. (*Pelmeni* is like dumplings, or rather like Italian ravioli, only filled with spinach and mushrooms fried with potatoes.) I still remember. They were so real I could taste them or almost pick them up. It was like a mirage. Starvation is insidious: you die yet you live. You have no food. There are no words to describe this kind of hunger. No, no words!

How can I describe the long hours I spent in Merri-Lokki! Sometimes some of the villagers would come and slap my face. Boris couldn't defend me because he was half dead himself; besides, I could have cared less. Pretty soon they realized that I didn't care and they left us alone. They thought that we were dying, and they were right.

Then Finland joined the Germans and decided to wipe out all the communist pockets in Finland. The authorities finally came to Kiskila and arrested the whole village. They came and liberated Boris and me, having heard what the villagers had done to us.

Before taking us to the hospital on stretchers, a colonel brought in some of the villagers and said to Boris: "Which of these men condemned you and slapped your wife?" Looking straight at the man most responsible for our ill treatment, Boris said, "I can't remember." I think this is one of the greatest acts of forgiveness I have ever seen in my life, that Boris could forgive the man who had attacked his wife. We were then taken to the hospital in Viborg, 40 or 50 kilometers away.

There we had to be spoon-fed for a while. Eventually we became strong enough to go and see my mother's estate which was on the river, on the other side of Viborg. When I arrived she opened the door and said, "Lady, what can I do for you?" She didn't recognize me. I weighed only about 85 pounds, and the tufts of hair still stood out glaringly. Starvation was still evident. Then she cried out, "Katia! *Cojass!* (O horror!) Katia!" and fainted.

She had a farm there, not a large one, but enough to provide some food. Everything was requisitioned for the war, but still, there was enough to eat. When we regained some of our strength, we felt we should go back to Russia to fight the communists. To help in this effort, the Russian authorities in Helsinki ordered us to go to Murmansk. To get there we first had to go to Narvik, a Nowegian town, and from there we took a ship to Murmansk. I still have a picture of Boris and me on the Norwegian boat which took us there. We were still a smart-looking couple for all our hard times. My shoes were made out of my mother's curtains, and everything we were wearing was made up of bits and pieces. The hat I had on was that of an Australian nurse!

That first night on the Norwegian freighter I spotted some jam! When nobody was looking, I gorged myself and ate almost four pounds of it! I was sick, sick, sick, sick! I don't know how you feel about sugar, but we had been without it for three years. How we had craved something sweet.

In Murmansk we had enough to eat, but when you have experienced starvation, you really never foget it. For one thing, you always want to hoard food. That's one unfortunate aftereffect.

A starving person can commit almost any crime without any moral or emotional reaction. One day while still in Petrograd, we heard terrible laughter coming from an apartment across from ours. We rushed in. A woman had boiled her child and was eating it! That's what starvation can do to you.

Yes, I remember all these things and sometimes I still dream about them. But I thank God for that experience because I can identify with the hungry. This is why it is so difficult for me to see people stuffing themselves with food. I always hear in the background, "Remember? Remember when you starved? They eat too much. They eat too much." This is why I have spent so much of my life feeding those who have no food. This is why I am so sensitive about food at Madonna House. This is why it hurts so much when I hear the West talk about food, never having really experienced its complete absence.

1920, with Boris, her husband,
on the way to Murmansk

6. Murmansk to Toronto

Murmansk is a Russian city which lies some 400 miles further north than Old Crow, Yukon, and how we got there is a story in itself. The surrounding terrain is not completely tundra, but nearly so, with only tiny trees because of the cold. Today Murmansk is a large city, but at the time of my story there was only a church surrounded by many Russian *isbas* made out of logs imported from the south. The town had only a few streets, and was being used as the headquarters of the Allied Army.

After the Communist Revolution, England, Serbia, Czechoslovakia and various governments allowed their nationals to come and fight with the White Army against the Bolsheviks. This army had three prongs. One in Murmansk, one in Siberia, and the other in the Crimea. These three prongs moved in the direction of Moscow and Petrograd. During our stay with my mother in Finland where we were recuperating from the horror of Kiskila, the White Army was advertising for recruits. We presented ourselves to the authorities in Helsinki, and very quickly were sent to Murmansk.

Upon our arrival we discovered that the Russian Army was in charge. There were British and French troops, Bulgarians and Yugoslavians, and also quite a few Americans. My husband and I were billeted in a small house but we rarely saw each other. He worked with the English Royal Engineers and used to go out on frequent forays.

At first I nursed, but when it was discovered that I spoke English I was transferred to the British hospital. God have mercy on my soul! I never experienced such rules and regulations in my life. The matron was practically God! You stood up until she gave you permission to sit down. Very strict indeed. Because I spoke English, I was assigned as a nurse for the officers. There weren't many; it was a small English hospital.

Well, I ran into a certain amount of language trouble. I could speak English but not American! One patient who was delirious kept shouting, "Shake a leg and make it snappy!" So I took his leg and shook and shook and shook! I shook it 20 times a night! I entered all this in the night book. It had one wonderful result: It made the matron break down and laugh! All the American nurses and doctors laughed, too.

Another assignment I had was to help out at the YMCA because Russian soldiers went there to relax. On my free days I visited them and translated letters, Russian into English and English into Russian. To thank me they sent what I thought was a box of candy and what looked like little peppermint sticks. I chewed one for about an hour. It wouldn't melt. I tried another. Nothing. I gave some to my husband. He chewed and couldn't melt them either.

One of the Russian officers said, "They might be some of those new candies you melt in hot water to make lemonade or something." I tried this but nothing happened. I called the YMCA and asked, "What kind of stuff did you send me?" He answered, "Chewing gum." I asked, "What do you do with it?" "You chew it," he said. Then I asked the classic question I have asked all my life about everything: "Why?" At the other end of the phone there was a profound silence. To date, no one has been able to answer my question as to why we chew gum!

Then the authorities discovered that I could speak many languages, so they appointed me to headquarters to serve as an interpreter. I worked both in the hospital and at headquarters.

This hospital was about 10 miles outside the town of Murmansk and it was reached by travelling along a narrow-gauge railroad. When leaving the hospital, you waited for the train in a little station hidden in the bushes and the hills. It was a simple building, also used for the storage of hay.

One evening toward twilight I was called from the hospital to headquarters to do some translating. I entered the little station to wait for the train. There was a huge pile of loose hay there which had been brought for the horses in use at the hospital. I sat down in the hay and started to doze off waiting for the train.

Suddenly I heard Finnish voices. In Murmansk, Finns easily mixed with the Eskimos, and Finnish was a common language. So there I was in the hay listening to this conversation when I started hearing them talk about "how we are going to use the dynamite." (For a whole week, headquarters had been in a panic over the theft of a consignment of dynamite.) "It's time to blow the whole thing up," one remarked. "How are you going to get there?" asked the other. The other answered, "We have made a road." They were communists! You can bet your boots I stayed as quiet as a little mouse. I said to myself, "Catherine, you will never get out of this station alive. If you make so much as a rustle, you're finished!" I felt a sneeze coming on as well, but fortunately I could control myself.

The train came. There were two small cars. They boarded the first, and I boarded the second. I brushed all the hay off and looked as demure as a nurse could look. I went into the first car and sat not too far from them. They didn't suspect that I could understand Finnish. They continued to talk.

When I arrived at headquarters, I was asked to translate some letters in connection with the stolen dynamite. I said, "Gentlemen, relax. I know where it is." (It was my moment of great triumph and glory!) The colonels and generals all gathered around me and I told them of my experience at the station. They arrested the men and repossessed all the dynamite. I received a decoration for this from the British government.

Eventually, Great Britain decided to bring the English soldiers home, and the other countries followed suit. Boris had contracted bronchial complications and pleurisy. The commanding medical officer (who was a bit in love with me!) suggested that Boris and I should leave also. "Your husband is sick," he said. "I can put you on the international ship to nurse the Bulgarians and the Slavs, and then I can send your husband with you."

That's exactly what happened. That's how we eventually wound up at Craigleith Hospital in Edinburgh. There I nursed the Slavonic, Russian and Ukrainian people for about six months. Time came for Boris to leave the hospital. In Murmansk we had been paid in Russian currency—the equivalent of 10 pounds in

English money. I was well paid for my work in Edinburgh. With this money we bought train tickets to London.

In London we went to the YMCA, and they remembered the work I had done for them in Murmansk translating for the soldiers. They gave us a room in the attic free of charge, a place where the servants usually lived. Boris was still very weak.

I had to earn some money. Many soldiers were returning to Britain, so for a shilling a day (25 cents) and tea with an egg or porridge thrown in, I worked eight hours a day on a treadle machine, sewing underwear for the Red Cross. Out of this shilling a day I managed to give Boris three meals a day, how, I don't know. The whole situation was really getting me down. I experienced a moment of strange despair, but nothing like the desolation that was to come in New York later on.

One day (I was only about 19 then) I was a little dizzy on the street, and I rested my back against a window. It happened to be the window of a chemist's shop, and the door was open. I heard a young woman, well dressed and with a lovely dog on the leash, say: "No, this perfume is too cheap. Only three pounds a bottle. I want something more expensive." To me, three pounds was a small fortune! I felt like taking a stone and smashing the pharmacy window. But I overcame my dizziness and went on.

Picture my daily routine. Our room was on the top floor of the YMCA building, and to reach it I had to climb a long staircase that ran out of carpeting near the top. The room was very cold and small. I was not allowed to have coal unless it got very cold.

I had to be at the Red Cross to sew at eight o'clock in the morning. The Baron slept in because he was still convalescing from pleurisy. There was only one bathroom for every three or four rooms, and it was outside. In those days there was no breakfast before work, but I left the Baron a thermos of tea and something to eat.

There was no tea or coffee at the Red Cross in the morning; you went right to these foot-powered machines, and pedaled all morning on an empty stomach. (A woman who came to Madonna House recently asked if I knew how to fast. My mornings at the treadle machine flashed through my mind.) Besides being hungry, I was still weak from Murmansk and Kiskila. How did I recover from TB which had developed from when the horse had kicked me? Every time doctors looked at my lungs, they found lesions—but they were all healed! It was a miracle!

How did I survive at the Red Cross? They gave us a whole hour for the "four o'clock tea." They had toast also, and I ate lots of toast and drank lots of tea! I filled up, but always kept some for the Baron. I always put the egg they gave us into a sack and took it home for him. It was hard to be hungry in London.

At a certain point we had to get out of the Y. So Boris said, "There's only one thing to do. Let's go to southern Russia and join that part of the White Army."

Well, I was agreeable because I was tired of doing what I was doing. But to get into Russia we had to go to the Russian Embassy which at that time still existed because England hadn't yet recognized the communist regime. So we went to the embassy. The clerk said, "You will have to see the undersecretary." We walked in to the undersecretary's office and sat down. Boris put his hand on the desk. The undersecretary looked at Boris' ring, which carried the de Hueck family crest, then put his own hand out besides Boris'. The undersecretary was wearing an identical ring. It was Uncle Walter from Riga!

When we finished embracing and exclaiming, he invited us to live at his house which was in the elegant West End of London. This was like a fairy tale—from the slums to the West End in the twinkling of an eye!

Uncle Walter and his wife were Christian Scientists. We stayed with them, regained our health with decent food, and eventually both Boris and I found jobs. Uncle Walter suggested that Boris could work at the embassy, which is what he did. He made about four pounds a week, and I was making two or three at a better position I had found (I had learned Pitman Shorthand). We decided that now we could afford a flat of our own. Finally, we began living normally.

We weren't happy though. The White Russian front collapsed, and the embassy had to close when England recognized the communist regime. We felt we were on the outside looking in. Boris started looking for jobs away from England, in the "colonies," as they said in those days. The first possibility was in India. But I had recollections as a child of the heat of Egypt and how my mother hated it. I said, "Not India." Together we looked at the map. There was only one place we liked because it had snow and was in a latitude similar to Russia—Canada. That's how Mr. Grub entered our lives.

He was a Canadian from Toronto who yearly visited England to replenish stock for his nursery, and he offered Boris a job. (Boris had taken the examination, and was admitted to the Royal Architecture Association. It was this accreditation that had influenced Mr. Grub. He needed such a man in his landscaping work.) We accepted his offer, thus bringing to an end our Murmansk adventure.

As I look back on this first part of my life, it occurs to me that I underwent a tremendous amount of pain at a very early age. When I consider that all I have told you so far took place before I was 20 or so, well, I wonder how I survived!

Until we met Uncle Walter at the embassy, it really looked hopeless for us. There were moments when I thought Lenin was right.

I found myself going to church all the time. I couldn't get to Mass except on Sundays but I would pass a Catholic church on my way to and from work. I didn't have time to stop in the mornings but on the way home from work I used to visit in this church. I still remember how it looked. It was very ordinary, but somehow I felt comforted, strengthened. I always had the intuition that there was something God wanted me to do. Notwithstanding the darkness of the London situation, I think I always had hope.

Arrangements were eventually made for our departure for Canada. We went by "boat-train" as it was called in those days. The train pulled up close to the ship so that passengers and goods could be easily transferred to the ship. They took me to the boat-train on a stretcher!

Now, why was I on a stretcher? Because, by the grace of God, I was pregnant. Unfortunately, I had decided on some last-minute shopping in London at a beautiful shop called Selfridges. I was shopping happily with the little money I possessed when lo and behold I fell down a staircase. Fortunately, there was still some time before we were to sail for Canada. The doctor put me to bed and said I had to lie flat on my back and be quiet lest I lose the baby. For about six weeks or more I lay in bed. That is why I was carried on a stretcher to the train, and carried from the train to the C.P.R. boat called the *Minnedosa*. In fact, I was on a stretcher all the way from England to Canada.

Our passage had been paid for by Mr. and Mrs. Grub. Boris would work for them for $25 a week, a tidy sum in those days. The Grubs did not exactly splurge. We went third class. But, all in all, it was exciting and quite adequate.

God took good care of me (and George, the son in my womb). At one point the propeller on the *Minnedosa* broke and in third class where we were the vibrations were so strong that the doctor and the nurse became worried about my pregnancy. Evidently, they conferred with the captain, because the next thing I knew I was installed in a first-class cabin right on the top deck. There were breezes blowing and a beautiful sight of the sea from every window. Of course, Boris was allowed to stay with me.

All things considered, it was a pleasant voyage, with doctor and nurse in attendance, good food and care. I can't say, though, that I arrived in the best of health. We landed in Halifax, Nova Scotia.

At Immigration we ran into some reporters and had to respond to some questions about our "identity." While we were in England, everybody told us that we should use an alias in Canada because "Baron and Baroness von Hueck or de Hueck" wouldn't be accepted in the New World. They said everybody detested titles. So we went to the Privy Council and changed our name to (or rather, were allowed to use the name) "Hook."

So when we met the reporters we called ourselves Mr. and Mrs. Hook. The reporters said, "That's not correct. The passenger list says 'Baron and Baroness de Hueck.' " We said, "Yes, that's true, but we especially made a point to acquire a simple name in Canada." The reporters just laughed.

The Immigration officers were very kind. Many people were on their way to British Columbia, to Saskatchewan, to work in the fields, or to become farmers. The Jewish people were met by a Jewish rabbi. The Protestant people were met by a Protestant minister. Catholics were met by a priest. Do you know who met us? Father George Daly, who eventually became the founder of the Sisters of Service who did such a wonderful work in the West. He had an assistant, a very thin young man called Father Patrick Dwyer. Can you imagine my amazement when, many, many years later we came to Madonna House in Combermere, and, lo and behold, who was the pastor of our little church here in Combermere? Father Patrick Dwyer!

Because of my condition, we rested for a few days in a hotel in Halifax. Boris bought a newspaper and when he began reading it I heard him grunting and showing his displeasure in many ways.

I said, "What's the matter?" He said, "Catherine, come and read this." He was reading the comics; we didn't have comics in Russia. "Look at this man called Jiggs. He is just a little fellow, and his wife, Mrs. Jiggs, towers over him with a rolling pin and makes him do everything she wants. This is terrible! I don't think we want to stay in this country. Perhaps we should take the ship back before it leaves the harbor."

"Let's go slowly," I said. "We'd better investigate this sense of humor. Maybe it's just the opposite of what it says." He slowly calmed down. For a Russian, this "Women's Lib" was a terrible thing. It just did not exist in Russia. Maggie and Jiggs were thoroughly disliked by the Russians here!

We traveled by train to Toronto. We sat on wooden benches and had a plaid blanket to cover me. The Grubs met us at the station and one of the first things they did was hand us a newspaper with the headlines, "Baron and Baroness de Hueck, First Victims of the Communist Revolution, Are Coming to Toronto. The Lady Is Expecting a Baby." Well, it was absolute news to us that we were news! We just accepted that as strange and as North American.

The Grubs acquired a little flat for us for $25 a month on Glen Road which is off Jarvis Street toward Rosedale. In those days it was quite aristocratic. We settled in, and Boris went to work for the Grubs at their firm, the Sheridan Nurseries.

Sheridan Nurseries still exists. The couple who started it were typically English, and they certainly knew their nursery gardens as most English people do. Their nurseries were located on the road toward Hamilton which, in those days, was all farmland and orchards. Boris did the landscaping for them.

It didn't take long for us to discover that $25 a week was not very much to live on in Canada; $25 a month for rent seemed very high to us. Some of our friends suggested we buy a house. To a stranger in a strange land, to people whose houses were handed down to them from their ancestors, paying rent for a house was quite unusual.

Our friends drove us to the outskirts of town, to a neat little house at 26 Nairn Avenue. The price was $2,500, and we could buy it for $20 a month. Beyond was farmland. We couldn't buy furniture, but people were generous and donated some.

It is very difficult to explain, but we turned out to be people of great interest to the Toronto public. We both were often invited to meet all kinds of important people because we were the first Russian refugees in town, and on top of that we were titled. We often wondered why we had gone to the Privy Council and had our name changed to Hook!

The Toronto of 1920/21 was very generous to us. When people realized that I was pregnant, I received 102 layettes! I was overwhelmed by that generosity but, of course, could not use all of them. I kept some for George and shared the rest with the poor. (I was already quite sure that I would have a son.)

A Doctor Galle, an Englishman, was recommended to me. A good friend paid for a private room for me in the Toronto General Hospital. During my son George's birth I yelled like a banshee (so the nurses told me afterwards). I kept crying out, "Dr. Galle! Dr. Galle! Dr. Galle!" My labor lasted 48 hours, both because of my fall and the baby's size—nine pounds!

I nursed him. We returned to Nairn Avenue and the Baron changed jobs.

Mr. Hayes, of the Barrymore-Hayes Carpet Factory, needed an architect. He hired Boris not only as a carpet designer (Boris had a very good sense of design) but also to help maintain the architectural splendor of the huge factory. Boris also did some designing on the Hayes' private home since they were millionaires.

We had many kind and helpful friends in those early days, and we were very grateful. Certain special ones come to mind—the Laidlaws who started the Loblaw Food Stores, and Colonel and Mrs. McLean, head of the McLean Publishing Co., publishers of many magazines.

One thing that puzzled us was our relations with the Catholic Church. When we were still on Glen Road (that is to say, shortly after our arrival in Toronto), neither Boris nor I wanted to move into a flat that hadn't been blessed. We were willing to stay in a hotel for 24 or 36 hours without a blessing, but not live in a house without one.

At that time we belonged to Our Lady of Lourdes Parish. Father Dollard was its beautiful pastor, and a very lovable man. However, when we asked him to bless our flat he answered, "Sure, someday I will come down and bless it. I will bring a quart of holy water to make it real clean of devils and such."

But I said, "No, Father, not 'someday,' but now! We can't move into an unblessed house."

"Why not?" he said.

I opened my big blue eyes and said, "Why not! You're a priest and you ask questions like that?" We came to a sort of impasse! He looked at me very intently, then decided to bless the house. Evidently I looked very sad. He blessed it and we moved in. That was our first encounter with what seemed to us strange ways.

A second situation of a similar nature arose. One day I met Father Dollard at the corner of Bloor and Yonge, a few blocks from the parish church. Like every good Catholic woman, I kissed his hands. After all, the hands of a priest are anointed with holy oils, aren't they?

Well, I almost stopped all the traffic. Father said, "Catherine, we don't kiss the hands of priests in this country." I said, "You don't? Why not? They are anointed with holy oils." He put his hand up as if to ward off my words and said, "I know, but it just isn't done." I walked away quite sad.

On a third occasion, we were at Mass one Sunday (I think it was the third Sunday after our arrival). Father Dollard was in the pulpit preaching about the Holy Name of Jesus. He was quite angry and was saying to the people, "Don't swear. . . don't do this. . . don't do that!" I couldn't catch much of what he was saying.

When Mass was over, Boris looked at me and said, "Did you understand what he was saying?" Boris spoke English as well as I did. "No," I said. "I didn't understand a word." Boris said, "Shouldn't we ask him?"

Well, we didn't go that day as we were still new and trying to feel our way around. But again on another Sunday he was angry and seemed to be chastising everybody about the Holy Name or something. So this time we went to his rectory and very humbly asked what the sermon was all about since we couldn't understand a word.

He asked, "Don't you swear in Russia by the Holy Name?" Boris and I looked horrified.

"Swear by the Holy Name!" I exclaimed. "That's impossible, Father."

"Well," he said, "what or how do you swear?"

I hesitated. "I'll let my husband tell you, Father. I'll step outside for a moment!" Boris told him. He laughed and laughed and laughed. I could hear him laughing outside. I opened the door and came back in.

"Well," he said, "I guess you poor children, then, didn't understand anything that I had said. As long as you don't swear by the Holy Name, you don't have to enroll in the Holy Name Society." He said good-bye with a blessing. He was still laughing as he walked away down the corridor.

Still another encounter with the attitudes of the Catholic Church in Toronto: Our first Lent in Canada arrived. Boris and I decided we would fast in gratitude for our arrival in this new country. There was so much to fast for. We were invited out someplace for tea, and several priests were present. Everybody was eating bologna sandwiches. Well, according to the rules, they were not supposed to be eating between meals. When the sandwiches were passed around, we only took some tea. No sugar, no cookies, no sandwiches. Somebody asked, "Don't you care for any sandwiches?" Boris replied, "We are used to fasting." They said, "You don't have to fast in Canada if you are working people, teachers, pregnant mothers, and so forth."

By the time they finished mentioning all the people who were excused from fasting, I couldn't think of anybody who was supposed to fast! This presented a little problem for us. I asked the priest, "All right, if all those people are excused, who should fast?" He answered, "Very few people fast here in Canada because it is so very cold."

I looked him straight in the eye and said, "Cold! I come from Russia!" That stopped him. He didn't know what to say or do. He looked at his bologna sandwich and said, "I am a working person too." I decided it was time to stop discussing the practice of fasting in Canada.

Boris became sick again and I started working. Quite a few Russians now began to immigrate to Canada from the Crimea,

Murmansk, and the Siberian front. The White Army had been repulsed by the Red Army and many people were fleeing Russia. We sponsored several hundred of them upon their coming to Canada.

Boris recuperated. He was hired by the Dominion Factory Company in Montreal, and he stayed in Montreal after that. This became a troubled time for our marriage. Both of us were moving hither, thither and yon. I began to get many requests to lecture, and so was away a great deal. Boris contracted other attachments, and we began to go our separate ways. I will have opportunity to speak more about this further on in my story.

7. Job Hunting in New York

My son was baptized in the parish of St. Clare's at the north end of Toronto. It was almost a rural area at the time, fields and farms. The parish priest's name was Father McCabe, and he was very good to me. It was a new parish. The good pastor saw me struggling with so little money that I used to help scrub the church and do other things for the parish. One day Father McCabe said to me, "Catherine, why don't you go to New York? You won't make much money in Canada. This T. Eaton Company job of yours (where I was working at the time) is a dead-end street."

It was shortly after World War I and veterans and their wives were taking up all the jobs. You had to fight this job situation. George was now about six months old and I did not know what to do about him. Father McCabe said, "You can leave George in charge of your neighbor until you are settled and get a little money together. She is a good Catholic woman with a child of her own." He gave me the fare to New York.

This was my first visit to New York. I remember coming out of Grand Central Station and being overwhelmed by the sight of New York. I had seen pictures of those massive buildings, but the actual sight was simply overwhelming.

I did the strangest thing. I stood outside Grand Central Station (I had very little baggage) and I looked at the immensity of New York, and said, "You do not frighten me." I said it aloud: "I'll conquer you." A policeman or a taxi driver, or somebody said, "Atta girl!"

I didn't have any money for a taxi, so I walked to the YMCA (or perhaps I rented a room for a day, I forget exactly). Eventually I landed a job as a laundress on 14th Street. The boss was a nice Jewish man, but the place was very, very hot. I started out doing sheets on a hot iron, and later was "promoted" to pillowcases. I had never seen anything like it. My pay was seven "bucks" a week.

I wasn't too happy. I had been making 12 dollars a week at

the T. Eaton Company, but I said to myself, "This is just a beginning."

I asked the girls I worked with where they roomed. They said Charles Street, the street which leads to the Hudson River and the waterfront. It was downtown. I asked, "Do you think I can get a room there?" "Oh yes," they said, "you can get a piece of a bed because one girl left."

That's how I met Ma Murphy, a good Catholic woman whose husband was a tugboat captain. Her boardinghouse was a three-story affair, with the girls on the top floor and her and her tugboat husband in the middle. Stevedores rented rooms on the first floor.

So I rented a "piece of bed," literally. There were three girls to a bed, six to a room, each paying a dollar a week to Mrs Murphy. I sent two dollars a week for George in Toronto, and kept four. Not very much, really, to live on.

All of us walked every day from Charles Street to 14th, about a mile or so. It wore out the shoes, but shoe leather at the Salvation Army was fairly cheap. You could buy a pair of shoes for 15 cents.

This was a strange period in my life. Every time we finished work we walked into a strange loneliness, a terrible loneliness. There is no greater loneliness than being in a crowd of people you don't know. The laundry girls and I lived in a profound, collective poverty.

It was as if Charles Street did not exist for the rest of the people in the city. You even had difficulty getting a priest to come with the Eucharist. (They were afraid of the stevedores getting drunk.) They did bring the Eucharist, but that's about all they came for. The church was very far away from us, even though geographically it was near. Nothing seemed to make too much sense on Charles Street. I guess when you live six in a little room and three in a bed, nothing much does make sense.

The ghost of starvation was always at my heels. When once you have really starved, you never really forget it. I don't mean the simple hunger people sometimes experience when they say, "I could eat a horse!" No. I mean the starvation of people who are so weak from not eating that they can't lift a finger. That ghost of starvation lived somewhere in me. I don't know exactly where it lived, but whenever I was hungry, it rose to the surface. It rose up and seemed to laugh. The ghost of starvation laughing! Hunger laughing! But that's how I felt sometimes.

In bed we at least had warm quilts. We talked mostly about food! The girls would remark, "Look, my belt is down one notch. I must be reducing." One very thin girl already had a tiny waist. She was still losing weight because she was hungry. Seven dollars a week didn't come anywhere near to feeding us. We used to talk sometimes about "sniffing" the food of the rich people and would go to Fifth Avenue with its big restaurants and walk through the alleyways smelling the good food. Then we would come home and talk about it!

Events seem to dovetail in my life. Here were two kinds of starvations. The starvation I experienced in Russia was acceptable because everybody was starving. The hunger here in New York was harder to accept because here only a few were hungry—and not much was being done about it.

The great temptation for a very hungry working girl in her early 20's was sex. When we walked out of the laundry every day, men were lined up on both sides of the street. They would say: "How about you, blondie?" or "How about you, red?" "Hey, blue eyes, how about a good meal and 10 bucks (or five or seven)?" Every night you had to run this gauntlet of men. As they taunted us, we could almost taste the meal in our mouths.

I think there are a lot of saints in the slums. I don't think God would have been upset if any of those girls had gone with those men. The hunger was extreme. We worked long hours and ate very meagerly. All we ourselves could afford was a meal at a "Sloppy Joe Diner."

Do you know where the food came from for the meals at Sloppy Joe's? From the Pennsylvania Hotel and other fancy restaurants. What people left on their plates was sold to Sloppy Joe. He put it all in a pot and served it with gravy on bread, or with potatoes and a cup of coffee. That cost 10 cents. For breakfast, the majority of us just bought a bagel on the way to work. The street vendors used to cry, "Bagel, Bagel, Bagel. Five Cents." And lunch? Well, it all depended. Most of the time we had bread with coffee or tea.

Little by little I learned the "mores of the lower classes." Class divisions surprised me in a democratic society, but they were certainly there. I must admit that I felt more at home with the poor than with anyone else.

For instance, Ma Murphy had a brother-in-law, Pat Murphy. Pat ran a real, honest-to-goodness waterfront tavern, with sawdust on the floor and everything, just like it used to be. On Saturdays he opened another room in the tavern and in the evenings invited us girls to come and have some fun with the stevedores.

He had one of those gramophones ("His Master's Voice" variety) that had to be cranked; then it blurted out fox-trots and waltzes. One night I was dancing with one of the stevedores and he started patting my fanny all over the place. So I said, "Why don't you keep your hands where they belong, on my waist. I don't like being pushed around."

He replied, "Lady, I know you're a good girl, because you live at Ma Murphy's. If you weren't at Ma Murphy's, and I didn't know the kind of girl you were, I'd put my hands on other places."

Well, that made me think a lot. This was new to me. The men I had danced with in the halls of Russia never acted this way. But I was learning, I was learning.

After a while I began to get quite weak. I thought to myself, "Why starve when I could be a waitress and eat decently?" (Waitresses, in my mind, had access to food.) I became obsessed with this thought. I had to leave Ma Murphy's because she catered only to laundresses. I had difficulty finding a job as a waitress. My money evaporated quickly. One night during this period I found myself on the Brooklyn Bridge, and I experienced a powerful temptation to end my life, the one and only time it has ever happened.

The water below was so smooth and inviting. Through the crisscrossed cables which held up the bridge I could see the sun drawing little pictures on the surface. I could feel the mood of the water, its preternatural power calling me.

I walked closer to the parapet, looked over the rails and underneath. Yes, I could squeeze through the wires. Oh, the water seemed so cool and refreshing. It was saying, in a language that only water can use: "What's the use? Seven dollars. Twelve dollars. Fifteen dollars. What's the difference? You have a son. You can't bring him up the way you should. Your husband is very sick; he might not live. It is all so uncertain. But I am cool. This is a strange land. It has no use for you. Come. See how the sun plays on my waves. I will rock you to sleep. What's the use? What's the use? You have lost everything."

The call of the water was very powerful. I found a space between the wires where I could slip through. I looked down and prepared to jump. Do you know what I saw? I saw Christ mirrored in the water! In a panic I stopped, turned and ran. I ran down the bridge so fast that a policeman yelled, "Hey, lady, slow down! You're shoving people around!" I was running away from the vision, which probably was no vision at all. But at that moment it was very real to me, and it saved my life.

I finally did get a job as a waitress, and in the shadow of the Brooklyn Bridge as a matter of fact!

So many little things struck me about New York. When I worked as a waitress we used to finish about two o'clock in the morning. The thoughtful taxi drivers of New York knew we had been working on our feet for eight hours. As we came out they would say, "Come on, kids, we'll give you a free ride. Who's going east, who's going west?" Free of charge, they drove us home. Through it all there was lots of joshing and good fun, but nothing off-color or sinful. I discovered so much good in these men, and I began to see another side of the face of America. You see the face of a nation in the behavior of its people.

Another waitress job I had which wasn't too pleasant was on the "Green Lines." In the subways of New York there are Green Lines and Red Lines, indicating eastbound and westbound trains. There was a pretty good subway restaurant at the Wall Street crossroads. From the Stock Exchange on ground level you could take an elevator right down to it. I was on salads, the boss having discovered that I knew how to make a mean salad dressing. (Today you can buy it at supermarkets, but not in those days.)

It so happened that a Wall Street broker I knew dropped in. He greeted me properly, "Hello, Baroness, how are you?" We chatted for a few minutes, then he left, realizing I was busy. Well, the owner of the restaurant had seen all this. He quietly went in the back room and made up a little sign. I didn't see what the sign said, but suddenly there was a lineup in front of my salad counter. One of the waitresses said, "Go outside and take a look at the sign in the window." I did. It said: "Salads served by a Russian baroness."

That was enough for me. I quit that night. I didn't like to work under those conditions.

I was always a very supple, athletic person. I skied, hiked, swam, and did a great deal of physical work all my life. I landed a job with Bernard McFadden who was one of the first physical culturists, propounding ideas about vitamins, exercise, and organic foods which are so much a part of the present-day scene. In order to acquire this job I had to travel to Poughkeepsie, New York, where I was looked over by the personnel manager. I was hired and sent to their New York gym where I worked with overweight women.

The class changed every hour. To each new group I would say, "Okay, let's do the bending exercises." I would make them try and touch the floor with their fingertips. It seemed impossible at first for some of them to do it. But I made them persevere.

Another exercise involved making them lie flat on their backs and move their legs as if riding a bicycle. That was really something. Big, fat legs trying to move. Thus it went hour after hour. I think the only person who reduced was me! I would say to them, "Remember how we did it yesterday." They would say, "We don't remember. Show us again." And I had to show them again.

Also at that time I went twice a week in the evenings to a gym where the famous Rockettes of Radio City Music Hall trained. I learned to do the cartwheel and other acrobatic tricks. If you had seen me then you would have seen really solid, acrobatic stuff! I did very well, but it was quite an ordeal to become an acrobat. Everything in you is stretched to the limit.

When I finished my training I was a pretty supple and limber young woman. The Bernard McFadden people promoted me. I was assigned to the young and slender girls, teaching them the exercises I had learned, but I still had the fatsoes in the morning. I received a little more money, but it got so that I really couldn't continue. I was getting very thin, eating all that vegetarian stuff at their restaurant (it was part of the program). My oversized ladies were going down to the Chinese restaurant and guzzling ice cream and whatnot. I worked at McFadden's four or five months, then started looking for another job.

The place to go for a good waitress job was Sixth Avenue. The employment offices were also located there. When you walked in the personnel manager would give you the once-over and then say, "Okay, 10 per cent." You had to pay him 10 per cent of your salary for the first three weeks. When I walked in the manager looked at me and whistled and said, "Okay! Here's the address."

I went to the place indicated. It was a club providing not only drinks but supper, also. The boss showed me the outfit I had to wear. Black stockings (sort of old-fashioned but very cute), a black dress with a little white apron, and a white cap. I began serving supper.

It didn't take me long to discover that it was more than supper I was serving! The customers, mostly men, sat in fairly large cubicles. I went over to a booth where two men were sitting. One of them started pawing me all over my bosom and back. For this I received $10.

I quietly went into the bathroom, took off my waitress uniform, put on my own clothes, and walked away. I had served only one person.

I went back to the employment office and exploded. "Look, I am *not* porno material! And don't whistle at me! Ten per cent, nothing! I'm going to the police!" He tried to pacify me: "Katie, don't get mad. I'll find you a good job." "To hell with you," I said and walked out. I chalked it up as another "experience."

Things were pretty tough during that time. I was living then with a girl in Greenwich Village, at 53 Mortimer Street. She was an actress in search of a job.

What I want to remember about New York most of all is the kindness of people like the taxi drivers and the wonderful Jewish man who picked me up one morning when I was really desperate.

"Blondie," he called as I was looking at some food through a window, "why is your nose up against that window? Are you hungry?" "Yes," I said. He took me home to his wife and daughter, fed me, and found me a job. I will never forget those kind people. So, yes, the face of New York was rough and tough for me at my first encounter, just as it was for so many others, but it was also kind, very kind.

1928, Baroness Catherine de Hueck

8. Chautauqua

Life is really funny. One minute I was nearly jumping off the Brooklyn Bridge, despairing for lack of money and friends, crushed by all the tragedies that surrounded me, and the next minute, out of the blue, I was making $20,000 a year! How it happened is a very interesting story.

I was selling in the gift shop at Macy's Department Store. A little lady approached me and said, "I understand that you are a baroness." That was a surprise. Few people knew about it. "Yes," I replied.

She continued: "I am Miss La Delle. I wonder if I can be bold enough to ask you to come to tea at my house next Sunday. You must be lonely in New York." I thought this was an awfully nice invitation. Yes, I was lonely. I said, "Tea would be just beautiful." So it was all arranged that on the following Sunday I would go to her house for tea.

Imagine my absolute astonishment when, upon my arrival, I found 40 other people there! They had come to meet me. My hostess said, in her sweet voice, "I wonder if you would tell us how you escaped from Russia."

Well, considering the tea and all the delicious French pastry that was being served, I thought everything was quite nice. I felt that the least I could do was to tell them my story. I became very eloquent (I didn't realize how eloquent) and told them my whole adventure. They were sitting on the edges of their chairs, but I hardly noticed. Afterwards I thanked her very much for the invitation, said good-bye, and the following Monday again punched the time clock at Macy's.

Around 11:30 or so Miss La Delle arrived. "I would like to invite you for lunch," she announced. That suited me fine. My lunch hour was from 12 to one. She waited for me, then off we went.

During our meal she said, "Baroness, I have come to make you an offer." She presented me with her card. She was a talent scout for the Chautauqua. Well, at that time I had never heard of the Chautauqua, so I really didn't know what her offer entailed. She said, "I would like you to start this September lecturing on the Redpath circuit of the Chautauqua." The Redpath circuit began in Sudbury, Ontario, ran through Canada into Oregon, California, then back again through Kansas City and ended in Chicago. Other circuits took in other areas of the country.

What was the Chautauqua? On Lake Chautauqua in lower New York State a group of Protestant educators, ministers and artists had come together. They were concerned about the fact that in rural America and Canada women often were plagued by "cabin fever" over the long, long winters. There was absolutely nothing for them to do for months on end. The situation was especially acute in sparsely settled areas. There was no radio or TV then, and the women just couldn't stand it.

For the men it was easier. Their work kept them busy. For both men and women there were the occasional barn dance and evangelical meeting. But these were few and far between. The founders of the Chautauqua thought it would be a good idea to bring shows, wholesome entertainment, music, culture to the backwoods of Canada and the U.S.A. And they meant backwoods. Their policy was never to go to towns with a population larger than 10,000.

The way they operated was very simple. They sent scouts ahead of time to see the town merchants and sell them the idea of helping to finance the venture. After all, the coming of the Chautauqua to town would be very profitable for business. The Chautauqua group brought the tent and the talent. Generally, those little towns had no large halls. So a tent was erected, big enough to hold about 500 people.

Then there was the program. Monday the Baroness de Hueck might lecture in the afternoon. Monday night there might be a symphony concert. Tuesday a play like *Seventh Heaven*, which was very popular at the time on Broadway. These plays, lectures, variety shows and concerts filled the tent twice a day for a week. On Sunday, Protestant religious services were held.

The merchants did quite well. They doubled their original investment. Families came from all over the countryside. Everybody and his brother would come to town for the Chautauqua. When in town, they would go to the restaurants, take rooms at the hotels, and buy at the stores. You get the picture? The merchants also had the satisfaction of knowing that they were helping to bring culture to the people even as they were relieving them of their money! It was a sort of 50-50 proposition! And it was a good thing. Madame Schumann-Heink, as well as many other really good artists, sang in these small towns. The two Broadway plays each week were always excellent.

We traveled in automobiles. Our engagements were often 200 or more miles apart. I would appear on Monday in town A, on Tuesday in town B, on Wednesday in town C, and so on down the line. We lodged with local families. Rarely did we sleep at the hotels (which were terribly inadequate anyhow, especially on the prairies).

Miss La Delle offered me $100 a week, all expenses paid, if I would lecture on the Redpath circuit. "I certainly am interested," I told her, "but I have to talk to some of my family first."

The first person I went to see was Father Martin Scott, my spiritual director, the celebrated Jesuit writer who lived on 16th Street. I was perturbed. "Is this Chautauqua business maybe a white-slave traffic of some kind?" I asked. I never heard Father laugh so hard. Tears were rolling down his cheeks.

"Catherine," he said, "the Chautauqua is very, very proper, and one of the most moral organizations you'll ever see. You are not going to be allowed to drink or smoke." (This latter was particularly tragic for me!) "If you do smoke, you'll have to hide. God forbid that with the Chautauqua you should smoke in public!"

I saw Miss La Delle and agreed to take the job. She asked me to wear a Russian costume, not necessarily during my lectures, but afterwards, for the audience. She proceeded to make all the arrangements for my new venture.

It was exciting—$100 a week when I was only making $12. It seemed like discovering the lost mines of Eldorado! I wrote the

Baron. He was excited, too. Everyone was excited! This was real money, something you could feel and depend on.

I went to the five-and-dime store and bought a pile of glass pearls. Then I went to Macy's and, at a discount, purchased a sort of silver lame at a very reasonable price. I made myself a real Russian costume.

I also needed an evening dress for the lecture itself. Do you know where I obtained the material? I had no money, but it didn't cost me anything—only the thread. I went to a priest I knew. In the old days, at funerals, the coffin was covered with a black pall. He gave me one! I took the cross off and made myself a dress, a black velvet dress. On stage, black is very effective for a blonde girl! Every time I put it on I prayed for the holy souls whose coffins it had covered. I am probably the only person in the whole history of the church who had made an evening dress out of a funeral pall. I think that's neat.

So I was ready. I had my velvet evening dress, my Russian costume; a whole ensemble that only cost me $3.50. I wasn't exactly a smash, but I was dressed adequately for the job.

I packed my little bag and went to Grand Central Station to catch the train to Sudbury. I settled comfortably in a sleeper but was unable to sleep. I suddenly realized that I was on my way to a public lecture and had never had an elocution lesson in my life. I said to myself, "Katie, how could you possibly have signed that contract! You can't speak in front of crowds." Miss La Delle reassured me, "Just speak to them as you spoke to us at our first tea." All well and good, but the thought of the crowds frightened me. She said that possibly there might be three or four hundred people! The joy of $100 suddenly vanished.

We arrived in Sudbury and, sure enough, the manager was there at the station to welcome me. I was installed at the hotel where the lecture would take place. On the way into the station I noticed the telephone poles plastered with handbills *with my picture on them.* I was in my Russian costume and "Baroness de Hueck" was written in bold letters underneath. I said to myself, "Thanks be to God my mother and father will never see these handbills." They would have ripped the posters off the poles. Publicity of this kind does not become gentlefolk. But this was America!

Finally, the day and the hour arrived when I stepped onto the stage. You must remember that, in the minds of Canadians and Americans, the Russian Revolution had happened only yesterday. Boris and I had been among the first refugees to arrive. This was something special. The people had rarely seen anything like it. A real baroness! Other than the Queen of England, my audience had never seen a titled person, except perhaps the Governor General.

Well, here comes this cute blonde in a black dress. Your heart would melt right away, wouldn't it? I didn't realize all this at that first appearance. It would take me years before I myself understood the impact of my stage presence.

I began to talk. My opening sentence was, "I was brought up on a farm." Not that the people of Sudbury were farmers, but, after all, this was rural Canada. I continued: "I didn't stay on the farm very long." Then I very quickly described my trips around the world with my family, coming even more quickly to the Revolution. This is what they had been waiting for.

When I spoke on the stage for the first time of what had actually happened, I began to cry. The whole audience cried with me. I became an instant success. Afterwards, as the manager escorted me to my room, he whispered, "If you can cry every day, we certainly would be glad to pay you $300 a week." I said, "I'm afraid I can't."

"Even if I put an onion in your handkerchief?" "Even then," I said. I was horrified.

During my performance I had to switch costumes within a two-minute period. This was part of the contract. I arrived on stage wearing my black dress, told my story, and then how happy I was to be in Canada (or America), and then said, "Wait a minute." I went off stage, changed, and ended my lecture in my Russian costume.

When you lecture in a large tent you are competing with a great deal of noise. There are cows mooing in the pastures, and trains passing by. Cars were being cranked up, and babies were crying That's how I developed my voice—by competing with all those noises!

Thus started my career in the Chautauqua. Every day, or almost every day, I traveled several hundred miles by car (or sometimes by train). I had to know how to drive. When I started in the U.S. part of the circuit I traveled with a string orchestra. It performed in the afternoon, and I spoke in the evening. We had an eight-passenger car which had an especially large trunk to accommodate all the musical instruments. This huge car required a heavy gearshift which I learned to handle very quickly. I did a fair amount of driving in the U.S., but in Canada I traveled mostly by train.

By the time I finished the circuit in Chicago, I was exhausted. I had lectured every day except Sunday. Usually it was impossible to get to church because there weren't any churches. I lost quite a bit of weight, but made quite a bit of money. I sent money to Boris and to my mother who was now living in Belgium. I had also hired a Russian woman to take care of Boris and George, and Boris was able to buy a car. Then I returned to Toronto with a signed contract of $300 per week for the Eastern circuit of the Chautauqua for the next season.

As a result of this first trip, a very strange thing happened. I had been traveling through what you might call the "grass roots" of the two nations. It had been wonderful to discover Canada and the United States this way. I had stayed at many farmhouses in the various locales.

When Christmastime came I was in Toronto. From all over Canada and the U.S. I received 300 turkeys! I gave them to the Salvation Army and orphanages. Some of my farm friends had even sent me two! Wasn't that a marvelous gesture of friendship on the part of these wonderful people?

The next season I made the Eastern tour of the Chautauqua. It started in the Halifax area, proceeded south toward Boston, and continued right on down to Florida. Along this tour the well-known Leigh-Emmerich Lecture Bureau was waiting for me. I stopped in to see them and they offered me $300 a lecture! That's how I entered the major leagues of lecturing.

During all my lectures on both circuits I always spoke quite vehemently against the U.S.A. recognizing the new USSR. At the time there was a Russian commercial mission of some kind from Russia, but there was as yet no official recognition. I also often spoke quite negatively about Communism.

What I didn't know at the time was that Americans write to their Washington representatives. When I arrived in New York a man named Kalpashnekoff came to see me. He was the recognized head of all the Russian colonies in America. For many years he had been a secret ambassador to Washington, a member of the Tsar's CIA you might say. He lived in Washington, and we all trusted him.

He said, "Catherine (he had known my father), you are creating quite a stir with your lectures. You'd better be careful."

"Careful of what?" I asked.

He warned me, "There are all kinds of people around these days. If anything happens to you, just let me know." I wondered about what he had said, but very soon forgot all about it.

Shortly after this meeting I went to visit my friend that I had lived with in Greenwich Village. From New York I was going to Montreal to visit the Baron. One day the bell rang. I opened the door and in came a gentleman I had never seen before. He was very well dressed, with a beard, and spoke Russian.

"May I come in?" he asked politely.

"Certainly," I said.

He came right to the point. "I am So-and-So (which probably wasn't his real name). I came to warn you."

Surprised, I said, "Me? What for?"

He said, "I am a commercial attache at the Russian mission."

Oh, I groaned to myself, and my stomach fell down to my toes.

"You are a Russian, a Soviet Russian?" "Yes, Madam," he said, "that's what I am. You have been opening your charming mouth too much."

He then explained to me that many U.S. citizens had written to their congressmen as a result of my appeal against recognition of the new Soviet government. "We have kept a close watch on your propaganda against us," he went on. "Many people in this town vanish without a trace. I came to warn you. It wouldn't do for you to vanish like that, now would it? Good day, Madam." He left.

I picked up the phone immediately and called Kalpashnekoff. He said: "That's what I was trying to tell you, Catherine. They are on your trail. We will put a secret agent in charge of you for a few days."

For the next three days I had a man following me around. Believe it or not, I just couldn't stand it. It was almost better to vanish than to always have somebody following you around. I felt sad for presidents and other VIP's who have to put up with that kind of "protection." I called Kalpashnekoff and said, "Look, I escaped all the way from Russia. God is good and he will look after me. Get this agent off my back. Anyhow, I'm on my way to Montreal."

Often on these lecture tours I had men approach me who wanted to marry me. In one of the towns in western Canada a chap who was wearing a ten-gallon hat and cowboy boots came in to see me after my lecture. "You sure have captured my heart," he said, "and you can have it and do with it what you want. Please marry me. I look like a nobody, but I went to college and got me a Ph.D. But I don't wear it on my sleeve because I don't like it. Stupid things, colleges, don't you think? I am really crazy about you. The world is yours for the taking because I've got. . . well, let's put it this way . . . I've got maybe a million, maybe two, maybe more. All of it is yours for the taking. And I've got a mighty powerful farm."

I asked him how many sections he had on his farm (even though I didn't know what a section was!). "There are enough sections," he said, "to take us to Florida or Paris or any other place you'd care to go."

It turned out that he was one of those millionaires in Calgary who owned sheep ranches in Australia and I don't know what else. I told him that I was already married, and that ended the conversation.

I have not spoken much of Boris, my husband.

Sometime during those years in Canada we had acquired 120 acres of land near St. Margaret in Quebec. In those days St. Margaret was in the wilderness. The land included a small lake which was excellent for fishing. We built a house, planned by Boris and we spent our vacations there.

I loved that lake very much. I used to row out to the middle, let the oars just sort of float at the sides of the boat, and dream about things. For some reason I always seemed to dream about Russia. I don't know why. Probably because of the many birches which surrounded the lake, which reminded me of the birches of Russia. The white reflection of these birches in the water was very beautiful.

Love dies slowly if it dies at all. There were many difficult days between Boris and me. My life with him was very strange. I always tried to forgive and forget. It was like a refrain, "forgive, forget, forgive, forget." It was during one of these "forgiving and forgetting sessions" that we went to the little house with the lake. We didn't take George with us that time.

The house was not made of logs, just plain boards, and I distinctly remember it was unpainted. During this vacation the problems that beset us reappeared. I could not take it anymore. Something died within me. I don't know what it was. Forgiveness did not die. Forgetfulness did not die. I was still able to forgive and forget. But the source of this love that I had for him. . . . Did it shrivel up? Did it just go into a corner someplace in my heart and hide itself there? I don't know.

I felt that day I had to go out on the lake in our little red boat. I rowed to the middle of the lake and stayed there, drifting, the oars in the water making funny little noises. I don't remember crying; no, I didn't cry. But now, like that time before on the Brooklyn Bridge, I had reached a new frontier of despair. I don't think in my life that I have ever crossed over into despair, because I had faith. Faith keeps you from despair, I am sure of that. But in my vivid imagination which translates experiences into symbols, I felt the cloying closeness of despair.

It was a very strange sensation this "despairing business." Was it gray? Was it black? I cannot tell you. I think it was both. At the time it reminded me of the fog that comes up from the bogs in Russia. When you go gathering cranberries, and are out after the sun goes down, you can enter into that fog and really get lost. It's not like the fog of London or of a countryside. No. It's a dank kind of fog. It comes from the heart of the bog. It makes one think of dark, damp, cold places.

This kind of bog is a good image of hell, because hell is not hot; hell is cold. The fog from the bog makes you feel cold all over. At first it is gray, but then it becomes black five or six feet above the ground. Higher up it melts into a gray. It is a dangerous situation. In Russia, everybody who picks cranberries makes sure to leave the bog before the sun sets.

On the lake that day I began to feel despair, this fog, this blackish-gray cloud. I stayed away from it, and it stayed away from me. It remained at a distance, but slowly it moved toward the boat and engulfed me. It was a strange scene. The last rays of the sun still played on the waters. The birches were still visible, but this fog, black with despair, hovered all around me.

Once again it approached, like that time on the Brooklyn Bridge. Once again the water was cool and gentle, filled with sunny ripples and this time the reflection of the birches. What immense peace this beautiful water offered!

I stood up in the boat and looked, not at the fog, not at the despair, but at the water. It didn't appear like a grave at all. Sunny water. White birches. It reminded me of my childhood—peace, love, laughter. The beautiful water spoke to me of all these wonderful memories, and the sensation came over me that I was very tired.

Yes, as I gazed into the water I realized that I had been tired for a long, long time. I had been tired since I left home at the age of 15 or 16. Then I closed my eyes and thought about what the waters offered me: home . . . birches . . . sparkling sunshine . . . Russia . . . mother and father. I began to hear my mother playing Debussy on the piano by the soft light of the three-branched candelabra. All the while the water lapped gently around the boat, and the oars made funny little noises as they floated with the current; and the fog was coming closer.

Then a most strange thing happened. It's very hard to explain. It wasn't the sun, because the sun was going down. It was more like a shimmering curtain. It moved in folds, as curtains do. Suddenly, it stood between me and the fog.

I woke from my dreaming and realized that I was standing on the last bench of the boat. I hadn't noticed that I was standing there, and that somehow I had gone from one end of the boat to the other. But I "woke up" from my dream. Above all, I woke up from despair, and from the gray-black fog which vanished at the coming of the shimmering curtain. With great energy I rowed back to the house.

I don't know if love dies all at once. Maybe love goes into a drawer and hides somewhere in the corner of a heart. I don't know. But I knew that something was happening to me and my love for Boris. Eventually, at the advice of a Jesuit priest, our marriage was annulled.

Every time I look back on this episode of my life, I call it "The Lake."

My romances were tragic in the sense that I never completed any; I ran away from them. Several such romances, after my estrangement with Boris, will illustrate what I mean.

One day, in New York, who walks into my little igloo but Father Edmund Walsh, S.J., who at the time was head of the Near East Welfare Association. He had spent nine months in Russia for the Papal Relief after World War I, working closely with the Hoover Commission and helping to feed Russia. I hadn't seen any of his "feeding" because I had escaped; but the point is that he was loved by the Russians.

He said, "Catherine, I want you to lecture for the Near East Welfare for a while." I agreed. They gave me a large desk. I began lecturing on behalf of the refugees—the Catholic Arabs and the rest.

Besides myself, another lecturer—a convert to Catholicism—was hired. He was a descendent of Cotton Mather, very handsome and very charming. He earned his money mainly as a book reviewer for the *New York Times*. We both lectured for the Near East Association and were paid a salary. He talked about his conversion, and I talked about the East.

Pretty soon after our meeting he asked me out for dinner. Then he asked me again, and again. Pretty soon he was falling in love with me—or so it seemed. I was in the process of getting my marriage annulled, and wasn't really too interested in a love affair. But he was handsome and charming, and it was difficult to say no all the time. Here's how I put an end to the affair.

I was saying good-night to him when he invited me to "come and have a drink at my place." I didn't want to go to his place because I knew that it could end disastrously for me. But I agreed to go.

He lived in a very chic flat, and I noticed a ladies' room at the entrance to the building. When we arrived I made believe that I wanted to go to the bathroom. I ducked in quickly, picked up a telephone, and called Father Martin Scott. I said, "I am about to commit adultery if you don't do something!"

He laughed—but then stopped laughing immediately and said, "Get yourself to the Cenacle." So while this good man was waiting for me upstairs, I ran out, took a cab, and went to the Cenacle. It was two in the morning but I woke them up anyhow. Father Martin came the next day. That was the end of my lecturer friend!

Also, while lecturing for the Leigh-Emmerich Lecture Bureau, I met another man whose family owned an immense steel factory. He really "put on the dog" for me. Every other night he invited me out and we had caviar, $60 dinners, and things like that. I liked dancing and we danced in the very best places.

But I soon discovered that this man had a wife stashed away somewhere. He was, however, really falling in love with me and wanted to divorce his wife. Even when I went to Europe he followed me to my mother's house.

During those days I was in the throes of hearing the Lord say, "Sell what you possess . . . come follow me," and I was running away from him. One night, while dancing with this man, I heard laughter, a very gentle and kind laughter. I heard what I thought was the voice of God laughing and saying, "You can't escape me, Catherine, you can't." I pleaded a headache and went home. Some new phase of my life was about to begin.

9. Beginnings of the Apostolate

A priest asked me once why I left a $20,000 salary and everything in order to do something so absolutely crazy as to go and live in the slums of Toronto during the Depression!

Long ago and far away, when I was a child, I wanted to be poor. Perhaps it began in Our Lady of Zion Convent in Ramleh-Alexandria, Egypt, where a little nun used to take us first graders during recreation to a statue of St. Francis and tell us story after story about him. I was fascinated! He was rich and became poor! So I said, "Someday I will be just like him, and I will go and live with the poor." Thus a dream grew in my heart.

I always discussed things with my father and mother and I wanted to know why we were rich. Father answered: "God has given us money so that we can give it away to others." That made sense to me. I was a child, but I had a brain that functioned at times like an adult's.

Even as a child I was eternally giving things away. I gave away our silverware once. (When I read the story of St. Brigid in Phyllis McGinley's book of poems, I had to laugh because Brigid too gave things away. I wasn't as good at it as Brigid, but, according to my parents, I wasn't a back number either!)

My parents were eternally missing things around the house. I learned at an early age to share. Once I was unwilling to give my red ball away, I loved it so much. My mother pointed out my desire to be like St. Francis. From then on I had no difficulty.

I married, and this dream vanished a little. My husband was very wealthy and I enjoyed many luxuries, including a personal maid. When I went to war the luxuries ceased and I lived in very poor conditions. The dream began to take on more shape when I saw the slaughter and the killing. This dream was like a formless mass that eternally came and went. The dream always centered around poverty unto destitution. (Gorky had written a book about the destitute ones who lived even beyond the realm of poverty. I liked that book.)

Years passed. Then suddenly, out of the blue, I became poor and all things were taken away from me. This was strange: The dream became a reality. But it wasn't a voluntary poverty, something I chose of my own free will. It was thrust upon me from somewhere—from God—because God permits that sort of experience. In the twinkling of an eye we were refugees and had nothing. We fled to Finland from those who could have taken our lives. After all, they had taken everything else—gold, silver, stocks and bonds, furniture and clothing.

In Finland and America the dream was a reality, but it wasn't my dream! It was as if somebody had thrust it upon me. It was someone else's dream. As I have already related, I was very poor, earning only seven dollars a week. I lived with the poor, and was shocked to discover that in the richest country of the world there were such terribly, terribly poor people. The Russian in me understood that I was one of the *humiliati* as far as my new country was concerned. I was a foreigner, a nobody.

This poverty of being a nonperson was a kind of poverty that I had never expected to face in my wildest imagination. Many people in many countries experience this poverty, and it is a very, very hard kind to take. Yet, at the moment I realized that I was a nonperson, the original dream came back. I realized that I was poor. I realized that what I had said and dreamt as a child in Ramleh was taking place. There was no statue of St. Francis here, no birds, but I was poor. In fact, I was destitute.

But there was in my heart and in that dream a rejoicing, and yet something was missing. The "missing link" was my consent to it. I was poor in those early years because circumstances made me poor. I didn't go and become poor myself. It wasn't a complete offering to God. It was an acceptance of God's will, yet accompanied by the desire to get out from under it.

Yes, this was something quite different. I realized then that my dream was not being fulfilled in this way. I was just accepting

94

the inevitable and also accepting what I considered to be God's will and duty of the moment—but not too freely. There is a big difference.

Time marched on. I made good money, as a well-known and celebrated lecturer. And when I was rich again the dream came back. It was now clear and sharp. It returned slowly, as I read the scriptures and thought about it. I wrote the fragments of the dream on all kinds of little pieces of paper. When I finally upended my purse one day, out came what I call the "Little Mandate":

> Arise—go! Sell all you possess . . .
> give it directly, personally to the
> poor. Take up My cross (their
> cross) and follow Me—going to
> the poor—being poor—being one
> with them—one with Me.
>
> Little—be always little . . . simple—
> poor—childlike,
>
> Preach the Gospel WITH YOUR LIFE—
> WITHOUT COMPROMISE—listen to
> the Spirit—He will lead you.
>
> Do little things exceedingly well for
> love of Me.
>
> Love—love—love, never counting
> the cost.
>
> Go into the marketplace and stay
> with Me . . . pray . . . fast . . . pray
> always . . . fast.
>
> Be hidden—be a light to your neigh-
> bor's feet. Go without fears into the
> depth of men's hearts . . . I shall
> be with you.
>
> Pray always. I WILL BE YOUR REST.

At last I had come face to face with the reality of my dream, the dream as God wanted it, because he said, "Arise and go!" My heart was pierced when I upended my purse and all those slips of paper fell out. Together they formed the outline of the dream, the dream of becoming poor of my own free will, the dream of my saying "yes" to God and not merely accepting hunger and destitution.

95

Now I had possessions. Now I could freely give them away. I could enter a poverty that was without limits because it was the very poverty of Christ.

I started to try to "get my dream organized." It took me three years altogether. First, there were a great many doubts and difficulties. Secondly, about 90 priests I consulted all advised against it, mostly because I had a child. But God puts dreams into your heart and says, "Leave your father, your mother, your children, your relatives. . . ." Archbishop Neil McNeil of Toronto alone sustained me in my dream.

How did I start out? Archbishop McNeil had asked me to make a survey of communism in that city because so many of his people were turning to communism during the Depression. I discovered that 28,000 Catholics became communists, and I fed this information to the radio priest, Father Lamphier, at the request of the Archbishop. Somewhere in the Toronto Chancery files there is a 98-page report on the communists which I wrote and which Father Lamphier used regularly.

I had a very nice apartment on Isabella Street. It had a big room with a fireplace, and two verandas, one of which was heated. George lived there with me. I also rented rooms to an Italian singer. In the large, comfortable kitchen, three people used to come once or twice a week in the evenings—Grace Flewelling, Beatrice Field and Olga Laplante. We discussed the things I found out as I was going about this work of the Archbishop. I had submitted my vocation to the Archbishop, about living with the poor. He told me to wait a year. If, at the end of that year, I still persisted in my desire to go to the slums, he would give me his permission and blessing.

But the events of those days are dim in my mind. Do you know why? It's very difficult to explain. My mind is sharp; I see the present, the future and the past clearly. But in those early days I was wrestling with the Spirit—you might almost call me an "early Pentecostal"! They are wrestlers with the Spirit too. I was in the throes of difficulties. True, the Archbishop had approved my vocation, generally speaking. He had, in fact, told me I was 50 years ahead of my time. This much was clear. What was not clear was, Should I do it? Should I leave everything behind? Should I sell all I possessed? Should I, or shouldn't I? Should I, or shouldn't

96

I? When you are wrestling with the Spirit like this the things of the world become slightly remote and a bit dim. That's why I am hazy about those early days. For me it was simply a time of wrestling with the Spirit in my heart. Everything else seems secondary and not very clearly defined. Situations and events are blurred.

Since I was trying to obtain this information for the Archbishop, I had plenty of knowledge of who the poor were, and where they were. Sometimes I would give away a chair here, a table there, or some kitchen utensils to this person. Slowly, I *was* giving everything to the poor.

I remember giving the piano away and its finely wrought stool. I gave away some very lovely pictures and some cups and saucers I had bought at Eaton's. But the Archbishop said that the best things should be kept for George. These I packed and put into storage for him, as well as a samovar and my Russian treasures that belonged to my Russian period. All these were kept for George.

Well, the Archbishop finally did give me permission to enter into my strange vocation, what I would call today that of a "poustinik." I remember the actual day very well. Carrying my suitcase and my spring-fall coat I reached the room I rented a few days earlier. Inside there were only three nails on which to hang my clothes, and a broken linoleum floor. It smelled of cabbage, just like all the other houses of the poor. Years later, on a festive Promise Day at Madonna House, I was to recall, in a poem, my first day in the slums of Toronto. Repeating here part of that poem is the best way I know of telling you what was in my heart that day:

My hands were empty. I entered a small, drab house.
The smell of poverty, cabbage and other cooking of
the poor was in the air.

A baby cried somewhere as I walked up a narrow stairway and entered the tiny room.

The window panes were gray with dust, so was the day
outside. The single bed sagged in the middle. The
two chairs were rickety, unsafe-looking. The kitchen
table scarred with ink and grease. The floor linoleum
cracked in many places.

No cupboard for the new posessions that I had. Just
nails with crumbling plaster on the wall.

Just nails. And a shelf or two. That is the room
I came in. The room I knelt in that gray October
day. Knelt and pledged my life to God forever and forever!

There was no altar. Candles did not flicker. Neither
did they sing their song of flame, of love and death.

No priests were there to offer the Sacrifice for me.
Nor was there any music, for there were no voices,
young or old, to sing.

No altar linens, immaculate and freshly ironed by
loving hands were there. But, then, there was no altar
to lay them on.

Nor was a table set anywhere for me. With beauty rare
wrought by loving hands.

No. There was nothing of the sort. Just a poor, shabby
room, and I kneeling on a cracked linoleum floor!

Yet, I would not exchange that day for any day today.

For well I know! My first promises were likewise my
final ones. AND THERE WAS MUSIC IN THE AIR!!!

The cry of babies. The shout of children. The raucous
cry of peddlers outside. The sound of traffic. Heavy
traffic, that takes a shortcut through the slummy city
streets. A women calling to another across a back fence.
The laughter of young people and of a man.

All these blended for me . . . into a music of sheer ecstasy!
These were to be "my people." In each my Love made
love to me! It was Himself, who sang that day for me—
the exquisite, incredible God-made melodies!

There was a priest in my gray room. The Lord of Hosts.
Who is Himself Sacrifice and Victim! The altar? His
altar was the world at my door . . . and the one He would
make and bring me in the days to come! . . . All of it was
there—that day in my gray, shabby room.

There were tables set. One apart from me. Resplendent
in beauty. Set not with man-made things, but God-made ones!

That day, I drank from His Cup of Love. And ate from
Plates of Hope. My hands were filled with flowers of

Faith. And Zeal shone a priceless necklace on my throat . . .
ALL THESE—HIS GIFTS TO ME!

My ornate clothes were gone. I was bedecked in splendor!
The gold of poverty shone like a thousand suns from them.
The silver of chastity made moonbeams pale! The jewels
His love gave me in that gray room . . . on that gray October
day—beggared the power of men's words!

The room became immense! And thousands of voices sang
my wedding to the King!

I know His Mother was there, and she whose name I bear;
the rest I could not see, blinded as I was with ecstasy!

Yes, I would not exchange my wedding day to God . . . in
that gray shabby room . . . on that gray October day . . . for
any other day anywhere!

I praise His Name. . . . My heart sings gratitude . . . even as
angels sing before His throne, unceasingly!

For behold—the Pauper, who wedded me in a slummy street,
a crooked house, a shabby room . . . WAS A GREAT KING . . .
CHRIST THE LORD . . . AND I BECAME THAT DAY A QUEEN
. . . HIS SPOUSE!

ALLELUIA! ALLELUIA! ALLELUIA!

One has to understand that I was thinking of poustinia. I
didn't expect tp pray three days and work four days, that wasn't
on my agenda. But I had the idea of praying and working. I would
pray when God gave me the time to pray (which turned out to be in
the mornings). In the afternoons I usually went out to help others,
that is, after a while, when I got used to the people and they got
used to me.

Thus I went to live in the slums of Toronto, and began implementing my dream. A few people joined me there, and Friendship House was born. We fed transients three meals a day. Three
rooms were allotted to those who were not accepted by the Salvation Army and others. We took care of the poor in the district, and
of the children.

A stranger in the slums is not accepted immediately. I had it
easier because I spoke with a Slavic accent. This became a
passport to acceptance among the Polish and Ukrainians. I had

the same accent as they. I was poorly dressed as they were. All my earthly possessions were contained in a little fiber suitcase.

My neighbors were quite astonished that I didn't have any money, except for $25. I had to pay four dollars ahead of time for the monthly rent of the room. Yes, four dollars a month—a dollar a week! That was as cheap as you could get.

In the beginning I had to buy some food. There was a grocery store next door. I casually let the owner know that I would be without funds very soon! I had enough money to buy potatoes, leeks, onions and carrots to make soup. My landlady let me use a spot on her wood stove for cooking.

Then came a day when my last penny had been spent and I started begging with a little eight-quart basket. I had never begged before, and so was very shy. It's one thing to beg for others, but quite another to beg for oneself. It was humiliating for me whom you might call an aristocrat.

The people in the grocery store were very kind. They gave me potatoes, partly black, but as one clerk said, "You can cut the black part off." I could do the same with cabbage. Cabbage was very popular in Ukrainian and Polish neighborhoods because *pierogi* is a favorite dish with them. I usually didn't make it because it required flour. I also begged bread, which sometimes was two or three days old.

The great difficulty was tea. Grocers didn't part with tea very easily. In those days it came in tins and it was quite something to part with even a quarter of a pound. I used to say, "Don't give me that much, just a little bit." I had an envelope for the tea, and its contents lasted me a long time.

Usually, my food consisted of soup, tea and old bread. Sometimes there was no tea, just water. I confess very simply and humbly that I was continually hungry—there's no denying it.

It's distracting to pray when you are hungry. In the morning I used to tell the Lord that if only my stomach was settled, I could pray better. He didn't seem to hear me or mind. So I offered him my hunger. My stomach used to make noises—"whrrrrrr" "whrrrrr" all the while I prayed. He seemed to like that.

I gradually became acquainted with the people around me. They gave me things sometimes when I helped them in various ways. I would look after a child and the mother would give me an apple. (You don't know what an apple means when you have had only the kind of food I had.) Occasionally I was given some *pierogi* and that was like a Sunday feast!

The bed I slept on smelled from the use of many people; but then, the beds of the poor always smell. The sheets were rough. The blanket was very thin but I had my coat to keep me warm. I often wished I could get a hot water bottle someplace. But I decided that nobody else on Portland Street had a hot water bottle, so why should I? I didn't get one.

I had enough food to eat, but never enough to be completely filled. A beggar really cannot beg too much. Beggars must be humble; beggars cannot be choosers; beggars cannot, for instance, ask for a chocolate bar! It just isn't done. Beggars can ask for bread, for tea, perhaps even coffee. They can ask for cabbage, potatoes and carrots. But they cannot ask for butter. That's a luxury. Nor meat.

Begging is a "look-see" from an entirely different angle of life. Even when I was working at seven dollars a week in a laundry, if I felt like buying a pound of butter, I could do so. True, I would have less money for other things, but it's different buying things with your hard-earned cash or begging for them.

The poor boil things, because it is the cheapest and simplest way of cooking. Frying requires ingenuity. Somebody might give you some bacon. (You wouldn't ask for bacon—that's a luxury too—but somebody might give you some.) You would keep the precious fat that was left over, store it away carefully. Then one day somebody else might give you an egg. You could fry it in bacon fat. Yes, when you live by begging you develop an entirely different approach to food.

Once I simply craved bacon because I used to smell it as I walked by the restaurants. I asked for some. They said, "Bacon! She wants bacon! What's the matter, getting up in the world? Ha, can you imagine that!" At the time, bacon sold for 20 cents a pound, so they just laughed me out of the place for asking for bacon.

This reminds me of a little Negro boy I met later on. He was standing in front of a drugstore, "sniffing" he later told the judge. He was one of the boys from my boys' club in Harlem and he had been arrested for snatching a purse from a fat lady. I went with him to juvenile court.

"What did you do it for?" asked the judge. The boy answered, "Mister Judge, I was sniffin' the bacon all morning. My ma had nothing, nothing to give us to eat. I was mighty hungry so I went sniffin' the bacon at the drugstore. Then I saw this lady. She had so much fat on her that I didn't think she would miss her purse." This boy was about 10 years old, and was called a "key boy." His mother, when she was gone from the house, put the key around his neck so he could go in and out.

I understood perfectly what he meant by "sniffin'." Like that little Negro boy, I sniffed it because I didn't dare ask for it, nor for any of the other "luxury items" that were found in the small, but not always clean, grocery stores in Toronto.

Food became very precious, and my appreciation for food grew immensely. I can understand better why a meal is an agape, a continuation of the Eucharist. When it is scarce, it has to be divided, and then it becomes very, very precious.

A man could beg for money, five cents for a cup of coffee. A young woman could not ask for money. She would be invited to a lot more!

I remember always being hungry. As you remember, I had been starved close to death in Russia and Finland, weighing only 82 pounds when leaving Russia. The ghost of starvation is very powerful. It twists your intestines and disturbs your sleep.

When I arose in the morning I would see my little eight-quart basket standing on the rickety table. I'd say to myself, with a sort of strange, half-awake fear, "Will there be enough food for to-day?"

Such a fear can only be conquered by prayer. I knelt by my bed like a little child and said to the Lord, "Lord, I'm sorry that when I was half-awake I doubted you. Our Father, who art in heaven, hallowed be thy name. Thy kingdom come, thy will be done on earth as it is in heaven. Give us this day our daily bread. ..." I'd stop there. I didn't go any further. That petition is very important to people who are not very rich. It was and still is very important to me: *Give us this day our daily bread.* You have to pray this with confidence when you have no money and you are surrounded by a seemingly adverse city. You say to yourself, "Who else but God will give me bread?"

Then it was time to go to Mass. There was always the Bread

and Wine to begin the day. If I hadn't been eating well, the Eucharist could make me a little dreamy, or even giddy. I thought about things then, or maybe it was God talking to me. I can't exactly say which it was, but it was good. Then I went to find my breakfast. If I had nothing left from the night before, I had to beg for my breakfast.

I remember those days. It sounds as if I was very concerned with food, but I really wasn't. I was trying to adjust to the lifestyle of a poustinik, of praying and working for the people. It was a time of both peace and turmoil within myself.

Next I cleaned my room. What was there to clean? It was a small room—a few nails to hang clothes on and the furniture I have described. The bath was always occupied, so the landlady gave me a pitcher and a basin. There was a sauna for the poor which I managed to use once in a while. It cost 25 cents. Although I didn't beg for money from anyone, sometimes people would give me money.

It would be a lie to say that I found the adjustment easy. Once I had worked out some arrangement for food there followed the wrestling with the devil. There was no doubt about that. It would be absolutely untruthful to say that I just moved smoothly into this way of life (praying all the time like a good little girl! Balderdash!). It wasn't all that easy. It was hard, for the simple reason that periodically I doubted my own vocation. I remembered the $20,000 salary I had left behind, and the car, the apartment and all the comfort I had known.

There also came a period of great distress when I couldn't pray at all. Then followed a period of great joy. I usually went to church and spent a great deal of time there. Nobody came in the mornings and I had it all to myself. I made the stations of the cross, said the rosary—all the things a good Catholic girl should do! Once in a while I used the prayers of the Eastern Church. I had a little prayer book I used, but most of all I liked to talk to God directly.

I went to help people wherever I could, although in those days I couldn't do very much. I would say to people whose children were sick, "Is there anything I can do for you?" Usually there was something to do. Sometimes I stayed overnight. Sometimes they had no extra bed and I would sleep on the floor.

That was all right. I have always liked hard beds, and I still do. This was a time of wrestling with myself, with the devil, and with God.

Father Carr was my spiritual director. I used to go and see him every Friday. He always had tea and crumpets and things for me to eat. He would ask what I did and how I did it. He probably thought I was a little foolish (but not completely so). Theology was on his mind. He would say, "Catherine, you need theology." Every Friday he gave me a lesson on Thomistic theology, which I detested! I would acquire the books and read the lessons ahead of time.

After each lesson we would have wonderful talks. He would ask me about some of my Eastern ways, and I would try and explain my Russian spirituality to him. He would say, "We must read some books on the Byzantine Rite." Then he would find a book on the Russian Fathers of the Desert at the Medieval Institute in Toronto. He would read and say, "This is very good, very good. Is this what you've been telling me? It's an impossible way of life!" I would say, "They lived it, why can't I?" It was hard to explain to a person even as wonderful as Father Carr what a poustinik was. It still is hard to explain!

10. Toronto: Rise and Fall

The "lone apostolate" I had visualized, with its deep personal identification with the poor (in a hidden way, as the Holy Family had been hidden in Nazareth) was soon scattered to the four winds. Three women and two men came to join me! I asked the Archbishop what I should do. "Get a bigger basket!" he said.

We were poorer than the poor. We lived with them and shared their sorrows and joys. This was only the beginning of the apostolate, and we were witnessing the first green shoots. Somehow we knew that we were the grains of wheat who must die to produce those small green shoots. None of us had the faintest idea of what kind of plant we were to become!

If you really want to know my own feelings, I thought (and I mean this most respectfully) that God was a little "crazy." I agreed with whoever said, "God writes straight with crooked lines!" The future was exceedingly nebulous in my mind, and at this time seemed to be composed of fragments of apostolic activities.

There was no denying that the needs of my neighbor were becoming for me a raging, stormy sea that threatened to engulf us all. At times it seemed as if I were surrounded by desperate voices, begging hands, and tired faces streaked with tears. I had nightmares about being suffocated and trampled upon by all these needs. I would often wake up in a cold sweat. This life was hard on us. The thing that amazed everybody was that we survived at all.

Food was a big problem. One day a wonderful priest, Father Joseph Ferguson of Warkworth, a rural district not far from Toronto, entered our life. He just "happened to drop in." He became interested in our work and helped by bringing us, every week, a tremendous load of food from the farms—potatoes, carrots, all kinds of vegetables, sometimes whole sides of beef and pork.

Notwithstanding his generosity, and increasing donations from various restaurants, the breadline kept enlarging with the years. The hungry families who couldn't get relief grew in number. Our own miracle of multiplying loaves and fishes (through our benefactors) never seemed to be enough. We didn't have any fragments to pick up. Neither did our own diet improve since we were giving everything away.

The meals included tea (often without milk) and sugar. There was porridge and bread, but never butter. Three times a week we had boiled prunes. This was our staple breakfast. For dinner there usually was a fairly good stew, which the men loved. Often there were more mouths waiting for that stew than we could fill. Again and again we fell back on soups for both dinner and supper.

We felt the absence of fruit and green vegetables. Occasionally we had a dessert of stewed fruit, but during the day the children of the hungry families usually walked away with the supplies of this precious commodity.

We did serve a four o'clock tea and an evening collation, which consisted of bread and tea. Thus we had five "meals" a day, but altogether they didn't amount to one square meal.

We all went to the seven o'clock Mass at the Polish church, although we belonged to the Irish parish of St Mary's on Bathurst Street. We made a meditation before Mass, so that meant we rose around six o'clock or so. Our retiring time was dictated by charity and the needs of latecomers. Often during the night we had to get up for emergency cases.

One night I was awakened to attend a little boy who had fallen through the rotten railing of a slum house stairwell. He suffered a concussion and a broken arm. His mother couldn't speak English and didn't know how to use a telephone. Such emergencies occurred three or four times a week; thus our rest was often disturbed.

In the face of such overwhelming needs, we could not take any "days off." Sunday was, for us, just another working day, feeding the poor.

We had a Brother Christopher (as we called the hoboes) who was a specialist in cooking. We called him Captain Pritchard and he was, in fact, a former sergeant in the armed forces. He was the captain of our kitchen. He was not a Catholic but he was a marvelous Christian. He stayed with us until the time of the "Big Trouble" (which I will describe shortly). His arrival released us from the kitchen, and you can well imagine we had many other things to do.

Begging for fuel meant that our premises were not always too well heated. The house where the women staff lived was a cavernous old building almost impossible to heat. Begging coal for it was a major undertaking. We kept the St. Francis, St. Therese, and St. John Bosco buildings warm, for the children, the poor and the Brothers Christopher congregated there.

Our own premises were not exactly neglected, but occasionally the Lord permitted us to experience the cold which the poor had to endure in their homes. There were weeks when we couldn't take a bath. The electric heater produced hot water, but the bathroom was so cold that it was better to go dirty than risk pneumonia. Periodically we gave away our bedding and slept on the floor in our overshoes and overcoats. Once I remember covering myself with a carpet.

All this may appear heroic, but I am not writing it to give that impression. I am just telling the truth so that future generations may know what the pioneers of Friendship House had to go through, and what the good Lord, in his immense mercy and wisdom, taught us in his strange novitiate.

Poor food, disturbed and uncomfortable nights, the inability to keep as clean as we'd like, an average workday of 16 to 18 hours—all this took its toll. We often had to go to a dentist who looked after our teeth free of charge. His name was Dr. Jim Talford. May his soul rest in peace. He was a good man and I always try to remember him and pray for him.

We continued feeding the poor. One day, during one of my visits with Archbishop McNeil, he handed me a newspaper with a format of only four pages. It was called *The Catholic Worker*. He told me that the woman who was responsible for it, Dorothy Day, wrote as I spoke. He said that he would pay my fare to New York so I could meet her. I took advantage of his offer.

It is difficult to describe my first meeting with Dorothy Day.

In some ways it was historical, because both Dorothy Day and I were pioneers in the lay apostolate. She had a wonderful influence on me. From our meeting a deep friendship was born which had, in a sense, profound repercussions on the whole lay apostolate of North America.

I found Dorothy in a storefront very much like ours, feeding a breadline in the same way we did—by prayer and begging. She was associated at the time with Peter Maurin, and she was publishing *The Catholic Worker*. She was just starting her "Houses of Hospitality."

She invited me to spend the night with her. I was to sleep with her in a double bed in a room that was filled with cots. People literally had to climb over one another to get to the beds near the walls. She was providing hospitality to women who were homeless due to the Depression. There were about 15 people in this one room.

As we were preparing for bed there was a knock at the door. A woman (definitely a woman of the streets), without a nose and with active syphilis, walked in and asked if we had room for her. Dorothy welcomed her like a queen and said, "Of course we do." Turning to me she said, "I have a mattress, Catherine. I will put it in the huge bathtub, and you will be as snug as a bug in a rug. I will share the bed with this lady."

Speaking as a nurse, I took Dorothy aside and warned her, "This woman has active syphilis. Make sure you have no cuts on your body. You might easily contract the disease through such a cut." Then I received my first lesson from Dorothy. Usually so mild, gentle and kind, Dorothy suddenly arose and in a spirited voice said, "Catherine, you have little faith. This is Christ come to us for a place to sleep. He will take care of me. You have to have faith!" I was dumbfounded. This was one of the many lessons she was to teach me by her witnessing and by her example.

We had a wonderful visit. It was decided that we would be the Canadian agent, if you want to call it that, for *The Catholic Worker*. Until 1936 we were exactly that. She arranged to send us several hundred copies. At first I worked at selling subscriptions, which wasn't too difficult. She was only charging 25 cents a year for 12 issues. Our staff and volunteers began selling this paper at all the Catholic churches in Toronto. Because our Friendship House address was stamped on each paper, *The Catholic Worker* brought us many new friends; it also did a great deal to combat communism.

Our two apostolates gradually grew closer. I visited Dorothy every time my lecture tours took me to the States. She and Peter Maurin often visited Friendship House in Canada. I remember one visit when our whole neighborhood was startled by our Yankee friends arriving in an ambulance with a huge red cross painted on the side. The *Worker* had been given this ambulance, and it used it as a cheap means of transportation. There is no denying that this constant and early contact between us brought us closer together and helped to clarify our apostolates. Through Dorothy I also made contact with many wonderful and important people.

One of these was Father Paul Furfey. Dorothy recommended that he come and see me and meet our pioneers. He was then professor of sociology at Catholic University and he was to play a large role in our apostolate. A warm friendship grew between us, and eventually he became my spiritual director. He was filled with Dorothy's brand of Christianity, if I can put it that way, and, in the years to come, he was to play a great role in the lay apostolate of North America.

About this time St. John's Abbey in Collegeville, Minnesota, became a center for liturgical renewal. The two priests who were instrumental in this movement, Dom Virgil Michel and Father Godfrey Diekmann, visited Friendship House. They invited me to lecture at Collegeville and we too became apostles of the liturgy.

Father Gales, the founder of the *Catholic Digest*, also came to visit us. We used to have long talks. I think Dorothy had some influence in strengthening his resolve to begin publishing that now well-known magazine.

Also around this time Dr. Jacques Maritain and Dr. Etienne Gilson were teaching at the Institute of Medieval Studies in Toronto. They were celebrated French philosophers, and their thinking was to have a tremendous impact on the church. They visited Friendship House and enriched us with their genius.

In the first four years of our apostolate, when it grew so quickly, I really did not know what the next day would bring. Temptations came and went. God sent many holy people, both clerical and lay, to strengthen and encourage us. My soul truly blessed these good people, and I never forget them in my humble prayers.

One of my Russian friends wanted to learn about the Catholic faith, so I took her to see Father Fillion, S.J., the founder of the Jesuit English Province.

When he had finished talking to her he asked to see me and said, "Catherine, do you have a spiritual director?"

I said, "No, Father."

"Would you mind," he said, "if I were to be your spiritual director?"

I said, "No, on the contrary, I would love to have a Jesuit as my spiritual director."

He was my first real spiritual director, before Father Carr, and believe me he was strict! He trained my will as only a Jesuit can. For instance, he would bring me cigarettes and enjoy one himself. One day, he gave me a cigarette as usual. Then, as we were smoking, he said, "Catherine, this is your last cigarette!" He didn't give me another one for three months! That's the kind of willpower he believed in.

During the Depression I picketed Senator O'Connor, the owner of the chain of Laura Secord Candy Stores, for not paying proper wages to his factory girls. The Cardinal called me in and wiped the floor with me. I simply told him about the injustices going on and then quoted *Quadragesimo Anno* to him. "How would you feel," I concluded, "if you were me?"

I got along with the priests I've mentioned, but I must say the majority constantly threatened me, and I was afraid whenever a priest walked into Friendship House. They would accuse me of being an unnatural mother. They would ask questions like, "What happened to your husband?" "Why did you get an annulment?" "Why do you spend so much time with the riffraff?" When I lectured, the priests often rose up and challenged me, with the result that the laity began to get the impression that what I was doing was suspect. That's how the idea that I was a communist began.

My son George went to a Basilian high school. A priest there told him that he should associate with a better class of people if he wanted to prosper later on in life. When I heard about this remark, I cried, and I went to Father Carr and told him what had happened.

Father Carr, who was the Basilian superior, called the priest in and asked: "Did you say that?"

"Of course," the priest answered, "this boy should cultivate the right people if he wishes to get along."

I cried again and said, "Father, is that the thinking of Christ or of yourself?"

The priest looked at Father Carr and asked, "You mean you object to it also?"

Father Carr said, "I don't think *I* object. I think *God* objects."

One person who seemed to understand me was Archbishop Neil McNeil. I used to go to him often when I couldn't take it any more. He was a small man, and on one occasion two tears rolled down his cheeks. "Catherine," he said, "pray for my priests. They are hidebound."

Besides the priests, other things were tearing me apart. I was frustrated because my "lone poustinik vocation" had suddenly changed into that of a lay apostolate in the marketplace. I had wanted to be alone and hidden, to simply serve people in humility. But here I was again, a sort of public figure, a center of attention. This rocked me. I just couldn't understand why God had changed my dream around.

The gossip increased. It made no difference what I did or where I went, people gossiped about me. I was accused of being cruel to my son by exposing him to the slums. Priests were especially harsh in this criticism, and I was very vulnerable because I loved them so much. Their opposition was my heaviest burden. Sometimes I felt as if somebody were piling bricks on my back, and the bricks were getting heavier and heavier. I felt I would fall and be crushed by their weight. I cried a lot. I had terrible doubts for a year or two concerning my vocation.

I can look into my heart and say that I did not dislike any of the priests in Toronto who persecuted me. I had a profound pity for them because they did not understand. At the time I thought I knew what persecution was, but I had only begun to know. It was to increase in Harlem.

Some priests, of course, were wonderful, like Father Sommerville, and Father Manning in Ottawa, both of whom were studying at the university. Father Carr, my director, was a great support. But I couldn't help feeling there was something devilish about those attacks upon me.

I went to the Archbishop again. "I cannot take it anymore, Your Excellency," I said. He looked at me. "Get the crucifix above the piano and look at it," he said. I did, and I understood what he meant. The Archbishop was a wise man.

Priests were not the only ones. While shopping in Simpson's a lady told me that she didn't speak to "traitors." Once I attended a lecture by Dr. Coady sponsored by the Knights of Columbus. I sat by myself. What I want to stress, though, is that, through it all, God in his infinite mercy never allowed my faith in him or in his church to waver.

After a year or two of this I was plunged into the passion and persecution of Christ. Little by little, God led me through the stages of his Son's passion. The passion we read about during Holy Week is short, only a few days, but, oh my God, how intense!

First there is the garden and the sleeping apostles. How often I was there. The staff in Toronto was asleep; they didn't understand what was happening. They hadn't awakened yet. There were moments when I thought I could almost see the rock where Christ prayed, and the blood dropping to the ground.

Then the kiss of Judas. How many Judases kissed me? I lost count.

Herod's court. The Way of the Cross. Strangely enough, I never died when I was crucified. I always came back to life and stepped off the cross. No one could see my wounds, but they were there. Sometimes I would wake from sleep, look at myself, and say, "I should have wounds." Then I would fall asleep again.

This period in my life I would label "sinister." I don't know how I persevered. It was due partly to those few supporting priests; mostly it was Jesus Christ himself. I couldn't leave him. He too was suffering his passion all around me. How could I leave him? But, oh, the desire to do so was very strong!

The problems increased. A nun accused me of being a communist agent, and the devil's lies spread and spread. I was absolutely disgraced; it was the end of Friendship House in Toronto. We closed. Toronto's Archbishop James McGuigan (successor to Archbishop McNeil) did everything imaginable for me, but to no avail.

It was a terrible ordeal. Everything that had been built through me by God collapsed, completely collapsed, but the roots of faith grew stronger. How else can faith grow except by being tested?

I told you how I began in Toronto—a beggar who was not allowed to beg bacon or eggs or anything that was a luxury. I leave you now with a person who had lost everything—a good name, the fruit of all her labors, the house of the Lord she built—everything. What was left? A person who grew in faith like a tree that grows by running water. These poems reflect my feelings at the time:

Persecution

They crucified
me with their
words
today . . .
then
not content
to see
me still
and as one
dead,
Hanging
as limp
as only
those
who know
the kiss
of nails;
the
pain of
wood;
they
used
the sabres
of their
eyes
to hack
me up.

So now
upon
the wood—
behold
me
hacked

up
in chunks
big
and small.
Each chunk
pierced
with its
rusty nail
of hate!
yet look
and see—
I am
still
whole.
Still
hanging
there
nailed
to the wood
with just three
nails.

I am
a sight
for men
to see
and laugh
and jeer . . .
but they
know
nothing
of my ecstasy
of love—
and cannot
see
that I
lie
in the arms
of my love...
in utter
peace of trust
and obedience,
and flaming
love!!!

A Post

For years on end
I wandered through
Deserts hot,
Parched and alone.

For years on end
I climbed cold
Heights and
Measured step
By step
Abysses deep.

For years on end
I walked in
Loneliness too
Deep for words
In search of You.

Then quite suddenly
I came upon You
My All . . . my love
Standing naked
Against a whipping post.
Clad only in the crimson
Cloak of blood and pain.

You smiled, and
Bade me stand
Against the other
Side,
Untied, held
Only by the bonds
Of love for you.

I did, and the
Long Roman whips
Cut me apart
And clad me in
The crimson of
My own blood and pain
Yet mingled with
Some drops of Yours.

Because of this
I am still here

At the same whipping post
Of yore.
You are not here.
The drops are
Changed into
Ones of fear and hate
Yet defenseless I remain
Because you still
Mingle your blood with mine
Beloved.

Desert

The pain
Is fire.
Its weight
Immeasurable
Crushing,
Until
Blood flows
From all
Of me
Like wine.

What is
The use?
To breathe,
To rise,
To live
A broken thing?

The pain
Is fire.
Consuming,
Burning,
Searing,
A broken
Thing.

Yet life
Is not
Extinct!

Is this
The end?
Of strength?
Of being?
Or just illusions

Singing
Their
Hellish
Lullabies?

All is desert
Hot,
Burning,
Blood alone
Wetting
The golden
Sands.

Blood
From the
Crushing
Maiming
Of the
Tremendous
Weight
Of His
Immense
And endless
Pain.

Is this
A sharing?
And atoning?
Is this,
This
The price
Of loving?
Or is this
Hell?

Alone,
Deserted by all
The living,
Prone
Crushed
A broken
Thing
Lying
On dry,
Dead,

Desert's
Sands.

All is
Silent
Of death,
Of pain,
Of desert
And of
Sands.
Is there
No voice
Consoling?
No hand
Healing
The wounds?
Nor stanching
Blood?

No,
All is silent!
Alone
I lie
Bleeding
Painting
A desert
With my
Blood.

Praying
For death
But getting
The gift
Of longer
Life
Instead.

Somebody suggested I go to the Catholic Worker in New York. I did just that.

11. Assignment in Europe

Dorothy met me at Grand Central Station and escorted me to the Catholic Worker. When I came in they sang the hymn to confessors of the faith, since they had decided that that's what I was! I must say it was very consoling.

Dorothy had no room to put me up at the Worker, so she placed me in one of those horrible little flats so common around the Bowery. It belonged to one of her female volunteers (who wasn't home at the time). Since I had nothing very much to do I thought I would clean the place; it was such a terrible mess. The woman would be away for a few days, so I thought she would be happy if I did some cleaning. I washed and polished, and did the laundry. Everything was ironed and clean and beautiful for her return.

But when she (I think her name was Elizabeth) walked in, she exploded! "Who in hell has cleaned this place up? I want to be poor and dirty just like the people here!" She threw me out. That was something else again. I stood there on the street with my little valise and said good-bye, not without a few tears.

I went to 28th Street where the nuns ran a home for young girls, women out of work, and people like me. The sisters had heard about Friendship House, but I didn't tell them I had just been thrown out of an apartment. They gave me a private room about the size of a closet. It had a little bed and nails on the wall on which to hang my clothes. It was very primitive.

I finally went to bed and fell asleep. Dorothy woke me up. She was on her knees, crying and apologizing for what had happened. It turned out that the woman who had thrown me out had emotional problems. Dorothy took me back to the Catholic Worker to share her own room. She was on her way to give a lecture, and would be gone a few days.

"Catherine, you will be very comfortable except for one thing," she said. "Amelia will come during the night, wake you, and want you to say the 15 decades of the rosary with her. After that she will let you go back to sleep again."

I said to myself, "This is life at the Catholic Worker! I thought I had it hard in Friendship House!"

Dorothy added, "Two other women sleep in the next room. Sometimes they are a bit 'under the influence.' They might wake you up and want to sing 'Sweet Adeline.' "

I got the picture: 15 decades of the rosary and "Sweet Adeline."

Dorothy left me with a blessing. Sure enough, everything happened exactly as she said. When Dorothy returned, we all said the rosary together. She was doing this every day; I had to do it for only a few days.

The editor of Sign magazine, Father Theophane Maguire, heard that I was in town. I had written many articles for the Sign.

He phoned and said, "Catherine, come on over to Staten Island (where he lived) and we'll feed your face."

Believe you me I gladly took the subway, the bus, anything that was running, and hurried over. The only thing they were serving at the Catholic Worker was this damn soup. Soup! That was a euphemism! You had to chase two peas across a watery liquid for an hour until you caught them. There was never enough bread to go around, since everything was being given to the hoboes who were quite numerous in those days.

Father Theophane and two of his assistants received me.

He said, "While we are waiting for the steak (!), let's have an Old Fashioned."

I had never had one before, and I liked it.

Father asked, "Catherine, if you were in charge of the Sign, what kind of articles would you have?"

I told him, and we had another Old Fashioned.

He asked again, "If you were the Archbishop of New York, what would you do?"

I told him, and we had another Old Fashioned.

He said, "And if you were the pope today, what would you be doing?"

They were having lots of fun. So I told them what I'd be doing if I were pope.

120

Then he asked, "Do you want another Old Fashioned?"

"No, thank you," I said. "Then I'd be telling you what I'd be doing if I were God!"

We had a fine dinner. After dinner, liqueur and coffee, Father Maguire came up with this offer: "Catherine, how would you like to visit Europe, see your mother and write a series of articles about Catholic Action in Europe? We cannot afford to send you first-class, but we'll send you tourist. We'll pay you $50 an article, which you'll have to live on."

I said, "Sold!" without any hesitation. Anything besides going back to Toronto to live.

Before leaving for Europe, I went to see Archbishop McGuigan (in Toronto) and he offered to send me first-class. The year was 1937.

I went to Portugal first and stayed with my friend, Maria de Luz Caupers. We had first met eons ago in England at Our Lady of Sion, Nottinghill Gate. We had met again in England when Boris and I landed there after the Revolution. At that time she had been on a tour with her husband and children and we renewed our friendship. She had invited me to visit her anytime in Portugal. Even when I left for Canada, we continued to correspond. She was godmother by proxy to my son George.

The Sign had put Salazar on my list, so I had to interview him before anything else.

If I ever fell in love with a man at first sight, it was Salazar (Antonio de Oliveira Salazar, Premier of Portugal)! He was so absolutely handsome in those days that when he talked I could hardly hear what he was saying! He wasn't too tall (which I didn't like), but very handsome. He had a picture of the Sacred Heart and a prie-dieu in his office. He told me how he was running the country, then said, "If they don't like it, I'll simply return to the university." He was an economist, and he introduced the corporate state into Portugal.

This concept intrigued me, so I attended a session of parliament. It was fantastic; I had never seen anything like it. Every trade and profession was represented and received a hearing.

Take, for example, the poor fisherman. He catches the sardines, but then he is at the mercy of the middlemen. In this corporate state concept, however, things are different. The sardine

121

fishermen elect their representative, another sardine fisherman who knows intimately their problems and is able to officially represent them in the parliament. The factory workers who pack the sardines also have their own representative, and so on down the line—owners, consumers. Each special interest group is represented. Decisions are made based on the good of all. I listened, fascinated, for over an hour, as a friend on mine translated everything.

My friend Maria owned tremendous *quintas* (estates). She grew cork trees which mature in seven years. She also grew porto grapes; the wine she served me had been made by her grandfather. I have never tasted anything like it. It went down like honey.

Portugal was very poor, and the illiteracy was very high, especially in the rural areas. Maria's sister, Vincentia, had an apostolate to these poor people, especially those living in the mountains. She taught them writing and arithmetic. There was another interesting thing about Vincentia: She had been present at Fatima for the "Miracle of the Sun."

In her apostolate with the poor she had heard one day about some children seeing our Lady and that on a certain day our Lady was going to give a special sign of some kind. Vincentia was single and had that day free, so she took her car and went up into the mountains to Fatima. She told me the whole story, and I still shiver whenever I think about it.

Thousands and thousands of people were there that day. Newspapermen (who by and large were atheistic in those days) were there, not only from Portugal, but from all over the world. The children said that a miracle would happen.

The press sat at tables in the field, and Vincentia took her place just behind them. Suddenly the sun began to rotate and move toward them! She closed her eyes because the sun was so bright it was intolerable. The newspapermen began to run, but it seemed that the sun was following them. Suddenly it disappeared into an abyss, then reappeared two minutes later on the other side. It kept coming toward them, growing bigger and bigger and bigger. Vincentia fainted.

Vincentia took me to Fatima, and I saw it in its primitive state. Pilgrim-like, I walked up the hill to the bush upon which our

Lady had stood. It was on top of a little cave by a brook. That bush is no longer there because people constantly plucked its leaves to take home as souvenirs and relics.

I didn't touch the bush. Sick people lined up while a priest offered Mass in the open air. Then he took the Blessed Sacrament and blessed each sick person with the monstrance. Every once in a while somebody would cry, "I'm cured!" We slept under a tree that night. Vincentia told me that she also had seen our Lady. For several years immediately afterwards she lived near the shrine at Fatima.

I made a mistake, Portuguese-style. Lisbon is a beautiful city and I wanted to see it. As I was returning from my touring, I met Maria's cousin, a single man about my age. Maria had previously introduced us.

"Ah," he said, "what good fortune! Can I offer you an ice?"

I was tired and I said, "Of course."

So we went and had ice at a cafe. We sat and talked for an hour or so. Then he escorted me to the ferry I had to take in order to reach Maria's house.

When she heard what had happened she was furious. She nearly killed me.

"You can't do that sort of thing. You're a young woman and you can't sit with a man in a cafe. You are disgracing our family!" She went on and on.

I apologized and she finally quieted down.

Next, I found out a few things about priests in Portugal. I went into the kitchen in Maria's house once and saw a priest eating at the kitchen table. I just said, "How do you do, Father," and left right away. Afterwards I asked Maria about it.

"I wouldn't invite a priest to my table," she said.

"Why not?" I asked.

She answered, "Because he is of a lower class."

"Don't any of your people ever become priests?" I asked.

She said, "Some join monasteries. Some become abbots."

This conversation puzzled me for a while.

I visited churches all over the country. One day I was in Maria's quinta and she said, "We are going to the parish church." By the entrance of the church I saw one of the most beautiful women I have ever seen. She was beautifully dressed, wearing a red apron, a large, colorful skirt and a beautiful coif. Next to her stood another beautiful girl about 14 years old who looked just like her.

I whispered, "Who is that beautiful woman?"

"Oh," said Maria, "she is the mistress of the priest."

I didn't say anything. We attended Mass and received Holy Communion from him.

A few days later I had an interview scheduled with the Patriarch of Lisbon. I asked him about the priest.

"Well, Madame," the Patriarch said, "the majority of our priests have mistresses. This particular priest has had a child by his. I have his assurance that he will not live with her anymore, but I permit her to remain his housekeeper, which is what she was in the beginning. That's the tragedy of the priests in Portugal. The Pope doesn't want them to be married, but the Latin temperament is such. . . . I close my eyes for a long time and don't see anything. Then, when they are in their 40s or 50s, I begin to see. Then I suggest that they desist from all relationships."

So that beautiful woman was living with the priest as his sister. He was now in his 60s, so according to the Patriarch, there was no problem. The people seemingly were not scandalized by any of this. So much for the priests in Portugal!

From Portugal I proceeded to Salamanca in Spain. Father Maguire wanted me to investigate the Falangist Movement there. It was 1937, and the Spanish Civil War was raging. Generalissimo Franco had his headquarters in Salamanca, and that's where all the reporters were. They accepted me into their little fraternity. They were "dailys" and I was a "monthly," and it makes a big difference. I didn't have to hurry around. The "dailys" were always hurrying around, while we "monthlys" (and some "weeklys") could move at a slower pace.

I started to mosey around by myself. I went to visit the first foundation of St. Teresa of Avila in Alma de Torres. That's where I saw her heart encased in a glass container. It is pierced, like a small sword had penetrated one side and come out the other. Even though the heart has shrunk and is very small, you can still see the wound clearly. The doctors are fascinated by it. She lived with that heart, with that wound! The doctors don't know how she did it, but I do. It is the wound of Love.

I was allowed to go into her cell which was facing the Blessed Sacrament. The floor was made of cobblestone, and I tried to kneel on it. Very hard!

Oh yes, one more incident I remember in Salamanca. I went into the huge cathedral where the knights of old attended Mass on their steeds. When I walked in the door in the early evening I had a sudden shock. Christ was standing there dressed in a long white robe! He was looking straight at me and I started to run away. Then I realized it was only a wax figure!

I talked to many people. I couldn't speak Spanish, but could speak a little Latin, a little Italian, and a little French. I managed to understand.

The majority of Spanish cardinals and bishops were also in Salamanca, refugees from the war. I interviewed them and wrote a story which, however, was never released by the *Sign*. It is one of my great sorrows that I didn't keep a copy of that story.

For example the Cardinal of Madrid said to me, "Sit down, compose yourself, and listen. Like all other bishops, we received the encyclicals of the popes on social justice. But we were not interested and didn't pay much attention to them. We went our merry way as we have done for centuries, doing what we thought was best for the people. We forgot that Christ had given us a way, and that the popes were trying to show it to us.

"We were very, very sinful, and we still are. I want you to know that all the parish priests in Spain who are poor, and all the convents that are poor, have been spared by the communists. The rich among the clergy and religious have not been spared. You may be thinking, what are you doing here when you should be in Madrid with your people? Well, just pray for me."

All the other bishops kept saying, "Si, si, si."

I was flabbergasted at what I learned from these prelates. As I said, I wrote it up and sent it to the *Sign*, but Father Theophane never published it. Somewhere in the *Sign*'s archives lies an interesting story about the bishops of Spain.

A *New York Times* correspondent and I received permission to travel to Brunette, a town on the French border which had been recaptured from the communists. This Irish gentleman had an old-fashioned Ford, and he liked to stop at the *bodegas*, the wine-parlors, along the way. "Katie, me pal," he would say, "what we need is a little sustenance, don't you think?" So sustenance we got.

My Irish friend would try out various wines before telling the innkeeper what kind we wanted.

After a fair amount of "testing" I said, "I think *I'll* drive to Brunette."

"That's a gooooood ideer," he replied.

The trip was a hundred miles or so, with German planes periodically strafing the highway. It was some ride!

In Brunette I encountered absolute horror. In the first church we entered, we saw a large ciborium on the altar in which consecrated hosts were inserted in feces. My friend exploded! With his handkerchief he removed the hard feces and put the ciborium back into the tabernacle. He was a Catholic, and he wept like a baby beside the desecrated altar. His face was just covered with tears. I couldn't cry because I was beyond crying.

Next, we came to a cemetery, and again we were petrified with absolute horror. My companion sat down on a rock and swore as I've never heard a man swear before—deliberately, slowly, monotonously, in every way it is possible to swear. He swore in sheer horror before the blasphemy that met our eyes.

It was the cemetery of a Carmelite monastery. The women had been buried on one side, the men on the other. The bodies had been disinterred. Some were strewn on the ground, still in their brown habits. Others were naked, and arranged in positions of intercourse. It was a kind of surrealistic hell, and it remains etched forever in my mind. There are no words to describe it.

My companion turned to me and said, "Can you stomach this?"

I said, "We are going to kneel down right here in the midst of these bodies and pray for those who have done this."

He said, "The hell we will!"

I said "Yes, we will. We are walking on holy ground. These people have been martyred after death. This is blasphemy. We have to kneel and pray for those who have done this. It's the only way to purify the cemetery.

He looked at me and began to cry.

He said, "Catherine, you're right."

We knelt down and prayed.

We continued on and came to a hospital run by Carmelite nuns. We both showed our passes (he spoke Spanish) and we were allowed to go to the bed of a nun. She was about 20 years old, and she had been raped by about 15 soldiers. After they raped her they cut off her breasts and cut her thighs in small pieces, leaving the flesh hanging. She was dying, so they kept her under morphine. This time I fainted.

There was also a German military hospital in Brunette since Franco had allied himself with Germany. German planes had bombed Madrid. We stood in the middle of that hospital and announced that we were from America and that we were newspaper people. I have never heard such weird laughter. The Germans jeered and told us that Hitler was going to conquer America and the whole world. We just walked away.

As for the Falangists, they were all busy with the war, so I decided to go to Paris.

Security at the border was very tight. They told me to strip. I stripped to the skin. They put me on an examining table. A female doctor came and examined literally *everything* looking for gold. Then they allowed me to wash and put my clothes back on. I have never felt so humiliated, so depersonalized. I can't say that Spain was exactly a place where I wanted to stay at the time; there was too much horror. Spain was another country where I witnessed the breakdown of a whole era and saw the monster of barbarism painted against a blue sky.

I left Spain and traveled peacefully to Paris on the French train. I acquired a little room in a hotel, but I couldn't rest. I was supposed to investigate Catholic Action in France. But I couldn't just now. I kept seeing that cemetery and the dying nun, the hosts in the feces; I kept hearing the laughter of those German officers, their threats (which almost came true), and their sneering attitude toward religion and God. These are not the gentle waves of a lake. They are waves from an ocean—20, 60 feet high—waves that crash upon the ramparts of our civilization striving to break them down.

My lifetime has spanned almost a century. I have often been pushed by God into strange situations and events. I can describe the events, but how can I describe the depths of those experiences, what was in my heart and soul at the time? I cannot.

her brother Serge

1940, son George

12. Paris, Belgium, Warsaw

Eventually I started investigating Catholic Action. Paris was a center of the Young Christian Workers, the Young Christian Students, and many forms of Adult Catholic Action. I was also interested in cooperatives, credit unions, and the labor movement; Christian drama also held a special attraction for me.

I visited the "Little Brothers of the Poor" first because they were closest to my hotel. They all studied cooking and looked after old people.

When I called on them I was taken immediately to the kitchen. A Little Brother was preparing a beautiful cake—Parisian-style, like a torte. He was topping it off with a beautiful, real rose. Then he took the cake, and a big basket covered with a cloth, and got into a car. I went with him. We drove to the slums to see an old lady whose birthday it was. When we arrived he asked me to help him. He laid out a luxurious dinner from soup to nuts, including the great birthday cake. There was a white tablecloth and real silverware. The old lady was in seventh heaven!

While she was eating he cleaned the room and put everything in order. Then he asked, "Grandmother, is there anything you want me to buy for you?" From her small pension money she gave him a few francs to buy some things for the next few days. I sat with her all the while and we had a wonderful time.

Then the Little Brothers took me to their chateau. A millionaire had bought this castle from its impoverished owner and had donated it to the Brothers. Elderly couples from the slums came there to enjoy a two-week vacation. The furnishings were beautiful, the food exquisite, the grounds extensive and manicured. The poor people enjoyed it immensely. (The French, rich or poor, have good taste!)

Much later on, the Little Brothers came to Chicago to start a similar program. But when one of our staff went to see them and then told me about it, it wasn't at all what I had seen in Paris. Eventually they left Chicago, but they still exist in Paris and in other places. They are a lay group who make promises and have a priest as chaplain.

I especially wanted to visit the Companions of St. Francis, founded by Monsieur Joseph Folliet. His idea was to present Christian doctrine (especially in the area of social justice) through drama performed in the open streets and countyside. I telephoned him several times but he was away in Lyon and I couldn't get in touch with him.

One afternoon I was sitting in a cafe having coffee and croissants. The cafe was situated at a *carrefour*, a crossroads, and it was about five o'clock in the afternoon. My table was closest to the sidewalk, so I could see people coming and going from every direction.

On one corner there was a huge clock, and under this clock stood a man dressed as a typical workingman with a red kerchief around his neck and a *kepi* on his head. He kept looking at his watch and checking it against the large clock, then looking up and down the street. It was obvious that he was becoming more and more impatient.

Suddenly, from across the street, a *midinette* approached. (A *midinette* is a seamstress in a large, wealthy home.) As all French girls, she was dressed very neatly and smartly. She walked toward the man who was still looking at his watch. When he saw her he clapped his hands and said, "Ah, at last!"

I couldn't hear what they said afterward as the traffic was pretty noisy, but I saw them kiss long and hard as the French do. Then he put his arm around her and came and stood right in front of my table.

Suddenly, from behind my table, another couple appeared, dressed almost the same. One of the men said, "I haven't seen you in a thousand years!" "Yes, it's been a long time," the other replied. They embraced, then introduced their girlfriends.

A few people (like myself!) were watching this whole affair. The gentleman—his name turned out to be Alfred—who had stood waiting under the clock said to his friend, "Where are you going? We'll go together."

Jean, his friend, replied, "Yes, Let's make it a foursome. We're going to church. There's a special Vespers."

Alfred said, "To church! My heavens! You don't mean it?"

Jean answered, "Of course, I am going to church."

"Are you still a Catholic?" asked Alfred.

Jean responded, "Of course. Aren't you?"

"No. I discarded all that opium of the people long ago. I'm a communist now," was Alfred's answer.

Jean said, "That's terrible. Why did you turn communist?"

By this time a rather large crowd had gathered and was spilling out into the street. Drivers honked their horns. An empty taxi stopped to listen. Another empty taxi pulled up into a front-row position. Soon a gendarme came along and shouted, "Move along! Move along!" But he too became interested in the discussion. Jean was quoting from *Quadragesimo Anno* on the church's position of social justice. Alfred kept saying, "Phooey! Phooey!" every three minutes.

The spectators started to get involved. (You know how Frenchmen are!)

One said, "Now look, Alfred, Jean has a point there!"

Another onlooker countered: "Shut up! The only thing left for us to do is become communists!"

There was action in the crowd now, and many were arguing among themselves. The gendarme forgot to move the traffic because he was also involved.

He said to Alfred, "You don't want France to become communist, do you?"

Jean answered the gendarme, "Yes, Monsieur le gendarme, that's exactly what he wants."

Honk! Honk! Honk! The gendarme was oblivious to all the traffic being blocked. Another gendarme came along, started to direct traffic for a few moments—then also became involved in the argument!

When everybody was involved, Alfred and Jean took off their hats and said, "How do you do! We are the Companions of St.

131

Francis. You have just witnessed a performance whereby we try to arouse interest in the important questions of the day. Would you like to contribute a few pennies so that we can continue with this work?"

A hat was passed around and they received a sizable contribution. Then they started to leave.

I grabbed them. I told them I had been looking for them.

They said, "Come and have supper with us."

That's how I met the Companions of St. Francis.

I asked if I could travel around with them for a while.

They said, "Of course. Is it true you came all the way from America to find out about our Catholic Action?"

I said, "Yes."

"We are going to the Rhone Valley, and it will take a few days because we make stops along the way." They were working their way through the vineyards of the Valley.

I knew I wouldn't be able to go all the way with them, but I was willing to go part of the way and see them in action.

We went as pilgrims. Everybody wore strong shoes and had a knapsack. The first stop was some 20 kilometers from Paris. There were no vineyards yet, but they asked the local farmers if they needed any help with their crops. I think we picked green beans. At the end of the evening they put on a play in the village square, and all the people turned out to see it. The play had to do with social justice and the farm. I stayed with them until they reached the vineyards; they began to cut the vines and squeeze grapes. It really was heavy men's work which I couldn't do very well, so I left them there.

I had followed them for three weeks. Every time they entered a village they put on a play. They were very good. I wrote up their apostolate for *Sign*, then returned by train to Paris.

On the way to Paris I visited a Russian Catholic church that was in union with Rome. A certain Father Dominic, a Dominican, was the pastor. They were happy to have me. One morning I had breakfast with them and they were very interested in America.

Father Dominic said, "You must meet Berdyaev. Jacques Maritain and Berdyaev hold soirees, and the discussions are fascinating. Maritain's wife, Raissa, will also be there."

I said to myself, "Katie, you have arrived!"

Gingerly, and with some trepidation, I went to Berdyaev's home. I was fairly young, perhaps looking younger than I was. Everybody knew about Dorothy Day, but nobody knew me. When Berdyaev figured out that I was a sort of Russian Dorothy Day, he said, "Come and join us."

I answered, "May I simply be an observer? I have little knowledge."

He looked at me and said, "You call yourself a Russian! Dostoevsky and Tolstoy taught that those whom the world considers ignorant are the ones God uses. So, if you really don't know anything—which I doubt by the look on your face—then you are doubly welcome. You can teach us."

I sat there and drank it all in. I wish you could have heard them. There were Berdyaev, Maritain, Raissa, three other Russian philosophers, Father Dominic, and I. It was a fantastic discussion. Berdyaev was talking about Russia, and Maritain, the great Thomist, was asking how the Russian theology related to the thought of St. Thomas. It was marvelous. A deep friendship that lasted through the years developed between Maritain and me. Berdyaev invited me to return, but I was leaving for Paris and was unable to make it.

Later on I met Emmanuel Mounier, editor of *Esprit*, and author of the book, *A Personalist Manifesto*. I had gone to the office of *Esprit* and was told, "He is in his loft in Montmartre." I went there, expecting something very exclusive and professional. Climbing a flight of stairs I found myself in an immense loft, beams exposed and walls unfinished. In the middle of the floor stood a large battered desk. Who was sitting behind it? Mounier! Little, hard benches were scattered around, and seated on them were many different kinds of workers—from simple laborers to intellectuals. It was bewildering at first.

A taxi driver near the desk was telling him that the taxi business was the worst business in all of Paris. He told Mounier about all the injustices being perpetrated against taxi drivers. A secretary was taking notes. Mounier said, "Ah, *mon vieux*, I'll look into that."

Then a professor from the Sorbonne approached, and they launched into a deep philosophical discussion.

Next, a big fat woman smelling of fish came up to him and said, "I just came from Les Halles (the central market). It's terrible! You have no idea. A poor woman can't eat the way things are."

I moseyed around, talking to people. Then it was my turn. He stood up, shook hands, and observed. "Mademoiselle, you come from far away." (I had American clothes on.)

I answered, "Yes, I come from America."

He said, "How can I serve you?"

I told him how much I enjoyed his magazine; also that I had read his book and was interested in implementing his ideas.

He said, "I have heard of Dorothy Day and of you. You work in the slums of Toronto. Yes, Baroness de Hueck."

He had seen a little article about me in Dorothy's paper.

We talked. He said, "We must continue our conversation. Come and have a *petit verre* with me sometime."

We arranged to meet a few days later. He brought some of his staff with him from *Esprit* and we had a really wonderful discussion about his philosophy in the *Manifesto*.

Father Dominic introduced me to Helene Iswolsky and Mrs. Danzas. The three of us sat in a cafe as the latter told us about Father Federoff. Mrs. Danzas knew him in Petrograd, and through his guidance had embraced the Catholic faith. Prior to that he had joined the Catholic church and had become a Dominican priest. Mrs. Danzas and several other Russians became Dominican tertiaries. They were all arrested with Father Fedoroff and imprisoned in Solovetsky Monastery which had been turned into a concentration camp. They suffered greatly for the church. She alone had escaped. Thus, in Mrs. Danzas and Helene, I made two new Russian friends. We often corresponded. Later, Helene came to America.

I also met the Dominican publishers of Cerf, and the members of La Pierre Qui Vire, a retreat house outside of Paris. With all of these people there were fascinating and brilliant discussions, but they seemed very far removed from the humble slums of Toronto; they would prove distant also from the slums of Harlem.

Paris too had its slums. They encircled the city. Most of the people who lived there were communists, so it was called the "red belt." I wanted to find out what was going on there, so I applied for a job.

I went to apply for a work permit for a 50-day period. I said, "I'm Canadian, and I am stranded. Can I work for a while?" The official said, "You can speak French. You're pretty. You're blonde. Okay."

They gave me a permit to work for 50 days, and I found a job in a delicatessen. It was in the "red belt" but I regularly visited the Jesuits nearby. They said I was in a position surrounded by communists.

I said, "Communists! Ha! I come from Russia, remember? Don't talk to me about communists!"

My boss, the *patronne*, was merciless. I worked from eight o'clock in the morning until late at night. I wasn't exactly paid an exorbitant wage (!), but I ate. The tragedy was that I was pretty.

"Okay," I said to myself, "I'm going to get a communist boyfriend. What better way to find out what is really happening?"

That's exactly what I did. You wouldn't believe all the things I found out about the "red belt." The only problem was, my boyfriend wanted to sleep with me, but I didn't want to sleep with him. We would go to cafes and have a *petit verre*. There was a lot of kissing (what you don't have to do for Catholic Action!), but sleep with him—never! Nor would I allow him many of the liberties he tried to take.

"Keep your hands off," I said, "I don't like that."

He'd answer, "What are you, a nun or something?"

"No, I'm not a nun," I said, "but I've been married, and I don't believe in free love."

He said, "You're not a communist!"

I said, "Of course I'm not a communist. That's what I'm here to find out about. Convert me!" He was a nice guy in spite of everything.

Every evening I went to the Jesuits to report on what I was finding out. They kind of watched over me. When I thought I had acquired enough information, I left, vanishing into the night, as it were.

Paris provided me with a much-needed diversion from Toronto and all its miseries. It also enlarged my vision of the lay apostolate, the needs of the church, and indeed of all mankind. I had many exciting adventures there. Besides Maritain, Mounier, Berdyaev and the other people I've mentioned, I met many more whom it would take too long to recount. I was really fortunate to have come into contact with them. I left Paris and went off to Belgium.

Belgium was very pleasant, of course, because that's where my mother and brother lived. I stayed with mother and had a grand time playing tennis with my younger brother.

Belgium was the headquarters of the *Jeunesse Ouvriere Catholique* (Young Christian Workers) founded by the Abbe (later Cardinal) Cardijn. He suggested that I follow the workers through a day of their activity, and take my time observing them. It was fantastic. They got up at four every morning and assisted at Mass before six. They ate little for breakfast. Then many of them went off to work in the factories.

I asked. "How can you go to work without food?"

"Oh," they said, "we fast." (Not all of them did, but many.)

At the end of one week I was exhausted by this regime!

At night we went to Juvenile Court. I watched these young people rescue other young people. Unless the crime was really serious, the judge would put the delinquent youths in the custody of the Workers. The Workers called their charges *copain* (friend, buddy). They took them right into their homes to share the life of the household. Poor as they were themselves, they offered these youngsters the hospitality of their own homes. Such kindness often changed the attitudes of the youngsters.

Night after night I watched the Workers approach the judge and say, "I'll take my buddy home with me."

"Your buddy?" asked the judge. "How long have you known him?"

"Oh, I just met him—but he is my buddy already!"

The judge would release them into the Workers' custody.

I also watched them put out their newspapers. The JOC was organized into sections for grade schools, high schools and factories, and each section had its own newspaper. One team was assigned to look after the papers, and another to oversee their work at the courts. It was all quite fascinating.

At the end of the week, on Saturday morning, we didn't go to the early Mass. Instead we went to a place called the "chateau." No doubt at one time it had been a chateau; at the time of my visit it was a huge dilapidated old house. We had Mass there, then breakfast and a discussion session followed by a period of silence. I have seldom felt a greater intensity of prayer than I did in the chateau chapel. There were lectures at 10 in the morning, and at two and five in the afternoon. During the time in between, they prayed, and you could feel God. In silence, they took walks in the chateau park. They called this their "day of recollection."

There was good food, and beer (the normal drink of the Belgians). On Sunday we had a picnic and dance, with all sorts of other things going on. I participated in everything. Such was my experience of the JOC.

Next I visited the university students. They were more dignified and philosophical. They met in groups in the evening and discussed how to bring people to God. Quite frankly, I didn't find this group too exciting, but I'm sure they did wonderful work. I only stayed with them three days.

Then I went to the *Jeuness Independent,* a Catholic Action activity among the bourgeois. It wasn't too easy to strike up an association with them and get into these more prosperous homes. They finally received me because of my contacts with the JOC. This group didn't impress me too much either.

Much more interesting than the last two groups was the *Jeuness Agricole*—the Young Farmers. They had their farm chores, held meetings, and were organized into small rural schools. They were really Christianizing the farmers, and you could see they meant business. Farms in Belgium are close to one another, and small, so it was easy for the young farmers to form these local groups. The leaders of these groups held monthly meetings.

Finally, I studied the labor unions in Belgium. I was flabbergasted at how well they were organized. They reminded me of the perfect order in which a Dutch *Hausfrau* keeps her house. I also had the opportunity to meet Van de Veld, then prime minister of Belgium.

The American contingent at Louvain invited me to lecture there. It's the one and only time I ever received 10 gold pieces for a lecture. Evidently they were pleased, because they asked me to repeat the lecture in French for those who could not understand English.

Thus ended my survey of Catholic Action for the *Sign.* I wrote it all up for them, said good-bye to my mother and my brother, and returned to the States. My overall impression of Catholic Action in Europe was not hopeful, except for the Young Christian Workers.

Upon my return I said to Father Theophane, "They are the most hopeful thing happening over there, but they won't last long."

"What do you mean?" Father asked.

"The forces moving against them," I said, "are too overwhelming. No, they won't last very long."

I based my opinion on what I had learned in the "red belt." The world was heading for a major catastrophe, but the priests were bourgeois, with just enough education to separate them from reality. In most of the movements, other than the Jocists, something was lacking—real, honest-to-goodness action. There were too many discussions, just too much talking. It made me tired. I imagined that the Lord himself would walk away from those endless discussions.

I sit here in the open air, writing these vignettes, surrounded by so much beauty, God's beauty. It is autumn, my favorite season. Autumn in Ontario is a riot of color. It is as if God were spilling his fire upon the earth so that we could walk on it. Bright reds and yellows—thousands of leaves of every color. Yes, it makes me think of God's fire, but also of man's. Before I continue on with my story and tell you about Harlem, there are several experiences from the war which remain indelibly imprinted on my mind. Strangely enough, in these absolutely quiet and peaceful surroundings, with the sun shining on my face and the glory of autumn in my eyes and at my feet, I still think of the war.

I think of a little red schoolhouse in Russia; it was autumn then also, with the same colors. This red schoolhouse was not very large, but under the conditions I am about to describe, it assumed cosmic proportions. Children came to the school on foot, wearing the birchbark (lapti) shoes of the time.

But now, during World War I, the school had been changed into a hospice, a shelter for the wounded, the maimed, and the blind. It had become an operating room. There were four doctors in two rooms, using ordinary kitchen tables for operating tables. Men were being brought from the trenches.

I was in that little schoolhouse. Other nurses were there as well. At the time I was not a registered nurse, having only attended an intensive Red Cross course in war nursing. But nobody cared about credentials, the needs were so enormous. I was told to take the amputated arms and legs and pile them in a heap a few feet away from the house. By and by someone would pour kerosene on them and burn them.

I remember the first leg I was given. It still seemed to be alive in my hands. I fainted. Nobody paid any attention to me except another nurse who simply poured some water on my face. When I came to she said, "Hurry," because three more legs were waiting for me on the floor!

So I picked up a leg (it was still warm) and took it outside. Everything after that was a nightmare. It lasted about 68 hours without much resting or sleep. The pile of limbs outside became higher and higher—a mountain, as far as I was concerned. After a while I could barely lift those small pieces of human bodies. Each piece weighed a ton, and the 68 hours turned into a thousand years. Carrying human limbs around for 68 hours can age a young person very quickly. All those hours of walking inside and outside of a little red schoolhouse, piling human limbs one on top of another, can give a young woman an intense experience of death.

Then suddenly I understood. Many people are still hanging on crosses. I saw the soldiers taking Him down from the cross. Just as I was holding the limbs of these poor soldiers, so I saw Mary stretching out her hands to receive Christ in her arms. In order to hold him, she had to grab him tight with her fingers. I had to do the same thing in order to hold these limbs. They put him in her lap, and she had to hold him tight.

Yes, a little red schoolhouse where children learned their lessons, 20 steps back and forth, a small pile made of human limbs (or was it the dead Christ?). Oh, the horror of it, the absolute starkness and reality of it all! Sixty-eight hours that changed my whole perspective on life, changed me so completely that everything before that time paled into insignificance.

From this scene my thoughts jump to another, from 1917 to 1939, from Russia to Hitler's Germany.

In 1939 Hitler declared war on Poland. I was again back at the schoolhouse, only it wasn't a schoolhouse any longer. It was a street in Warsaw with all the buildings bombed out. The large table was still there, right out in the middle of the street, a table much larger than the ones in the little red schoolhouse. Two surgeons were working at one table.

How did I get in Warsaw? Again, I had been sent by *Sign* magazine, this time to find out how Catholics were faring under the swastika. I went over in July, but by September I was in front of this table in the streets of Warsaw. Between that July and that September, 100 years elapsed.

In Warsaw I realized that in Russia I had only been on the edge of hell. Now I was in hell itself. The *stukas* whined ceaselessly over our heads. All the able-bodied men had left the city; they had been mobilized. Warsaw was left to the old, to the children, to the babies and the women. The city was not prepared to defend itself.

The planes simply dropped their bombs wherever they wanted to. Each one had a different tune, and each tune wracked the mind as well as the ears. They made a cacophony of sound that became a symphony of horror.

Here again, as in Russia, we worked without ceasing. This time somebody else carried the limbs away while I helped the doctors. This time there were maimed children, women, and old men, not simply soldiers. Here too, the nurse made a little mountain of the limbs, just as I had done in Russia. Suddenly, the two tables became one table; then the table changed into a cross.

Maybe it was because I was tired, I don't know. All the while I was helping the doctor, I heard the hammers of strong men driving nails into the flesh of Jesus. I no longer saw tables, no longer saw doctors, no longer saw children or women or old men. I saw only Christ. I will never forget that sight—the incredible horror of it all. I wanted to pull out the nails with my own fingers; to take him in my arms while he was still alive and shout, "Stop it! Stop this carnage!" But I couldn't say it out loud, so I said it in my heart.

Relentlessly the doctors kept asking for sutures, and for this and that. There was no time to pray. The *stukas* danced in the air to the tune of the exploding bombs.

When I hear tragedy on the news sometimes I still find myself saying, "Stop! Stop this carnage, this inhumanity of man to his fellowman!"

A day came toward the end of September when a *N.Y. Times* correspondent said to me, "Enough is enough. We're all leaving and you're coming with us."

Certain memories come to mind about our departure, but

they are a bit nebulous because I was so exhausted from nursing. I had to go and see the British Consul who was representing Canadian interests in Poland. A sea of people was there, all claiming to be Canadian. Many of them were Jewish.

Because I had a Canadian passport I was allowed through immediately. I saw a very tired man dressed in his *schlaf-rock* (bathrobe). He apologized for such informality, but I could see from the expression on his face that he was completely exhausted. He spoke very slowly.

"I see that you are a bona fide Canadian. What can I do for you?"

I said, "Sir, I need my Polish permit stamped so I can cross the border."

Half asleep he lifted his hand and stamped my permit.

I said, "Sir, you are completely exhausted."

"More than exhausted," he said.

Then I was surprised to hear this quiet Englishman say, "Pray for me."

I found out later that he was killed by a bomb.

This picture fades also. I remember sleeping on the floor of a large hotel for the next few days. I only had a backpack, the old-fashioned kind you carry like a bag, with pajamas and some bread in it. Inside the bread I carried a Retina II camera. I photographed the women digging trenches, the hospital table in the middle of that street, the children, the destruction of Warsaw.

Then we were on the road, walking. I still have the good pair of walking shoes I used then. English, Canadians, Americans, Australians—we all walked together, especially the correspondents. The *Times* correspondents felt they had to look after me. I was the "Harlem girl." We were following the railroad tracks to Hungary—and so were the *stukas*. They destroyed the railroad tracks and many other buildings nearby.

As we were walking along we watched a young woman hanging out her laundry. She had on a green skirt, a red cotton apron, and a yellow blouse. Her little child was with her, holding on to her skirt. It was a lovely domestic scene—the beautiful woman dressed in the native costume of the Poles.

We were approaching a small station, and apparently she was the stationmaster's wife. We could see the red flags used to signal the trains, and the geraniums in the windows.

Suddenly, the *stukas* came fast and heavy. We all slid down the embankment as they dropped their lethal cargo on the station. When we came out of hiding there was no house, no green skirt, no woman, and no child. A newly washed quilt was dangling from the limb of a tree. My flesh still crawls whenever I recall this scene. For me, that quilt dangling from the tree was a prophetic symbol of a world that was coming to an end. It was a symbol of the new barbarism which was invading the world. It was a symbol of bombings all over the world that would destroy little people of all kinds as they were trying to live their peaceful lives. A quilt hanging from a tree and a gaping hole in the ground! A prophetic vision of the march of the barbarians.

When we arrived in the Carpathian Mountains in Czechoslovakia, it began to rain. What a sight we were! People of all ages, pregnant women, wounded soldiers, all refugees from this Polish holocaust, all oppressed in their souls by this calamity. How different life becomes when you have to flee to preserve it!

It poured. Few had any baggage. We had all left Poland with next to nothing. Almost everyone was empty-handed. Perhaps I had more than anybody, with a sack on my back, a pair of pajamas, and my bread with the camera in it.

We were drenched to the skin. It was September, and we were in the mountains, so it was cold. However, I don't recall one single person complaining. I often think of this march when I hear people complaining about the weather: "It's so depressing! If only we could have a little sunshine!" They've never been part of a refugee column. What does it matter what the weather is like! You're trying to save your life. It rained for three days.

It scares me a little when I hear people complain about the weather. They are like little children talking about nothing at all. Children take little things so seriously. "This is my doll," or "That is my bowl." Many conversations seem that way to me. Rain especially does not make me unhappy. Do you know why? Because the *stukas* couldn't bomb us in the rain! Bless the rain. At one point in my life, rain meant saving waters from the heavens you could drink, instead of death from the sky.

My mind is like a motion picture screen. I hear the voices of today and I often want to weep because people haven't heard the voices of yesterday, and they do not see the catastrophe that is coming. Unaware of the past, they cannot hear the voices of tomorrow, not see the evils of tomorrow which will fall upon them. Maybe someday they too will be soaked to the skin and shivering, and thus learn how to bless the rain. Who can tell?

We trudged on. Two people fell over a precipice. One old lady died from a heart attack. We left her in the hands of a local priest who buried her someplace in the mountains.

There was a young man with us on his crutches. His bride had been killed in Warsaw by the *stukas*, and as he was driving her body to the church for burial, he had an accident. His truck went off the road and he injured his legs. The police took his wife's body to the cemetery. His only desire was to avenge his wife's death. As we marched on, he became more and more deranged. He ended up in an insane asylum in Budapest.

I don't remember how many days we walked—a week or so maybe. Finally we reached the Hungarian border where a train was waiting to take us to Budapest. After being processed, the correspondents all went to the same hotel.

When I woke up the next morning I could hardly move my arms or legs. I thought I was paralyzed. The doctor came and said I was in a state of shock. I remember the maid bringing me food. After four days I was able to sit up and begin to walk a little.

I called my cousin Nicholas Makletzoff who lived in Ljubljana with his brother, who was a professor of criminology. This brother had escaped from Russia and was teaching in Ljubljana. We left together for Italy, traveled on to France, and thence back to the States.

1965, dressed as a
Russian pilgrim

at the door of
her poustinia

13. Harlem: No-Man's-Land

How I finally settled in Harlem is described in a book I wrote called *Friendship House*, so I won't go into too much detail of my arrival and settling in. But I do wish to describe here how Harlem was a no-man's-land for me.

During World War I, heroic people on both sides crawled into the area between the German and Russian trenches to rescue soldiers who were stranded there. Both sides would hold their fire when somebody was being rescued. This area was called no-man's-land. I have been a stranger in a strange land for many years, but I also have lived in no-man's-land for many years as well. I reached the ultimate no-man's-land when I entered Harlem.

No-man's-land has many different kinds of terrain. God alone knows how difficult it was to be a stranger in a strange land, but when Father John Lafarge invited me to Harlem I faced a totally new situation.

My parents, especially my father, kept us from developing any kind of racial prejudice. I didn't know what a "racial prejudice" was. To our family, everybody was a somebody. At no time did we distinguish people by their race, religion, or color.

I remember a conversation between my father and mother when father was planning to entertain a gentleman from America named Pierpont Morgan.

Mother asked, "Pierpont Morgan, who is he?"

Father said, "Don't you know? He is one of the richest men in the world."

Mother went on, "Of course I know that, everybody knows that—but what has he done?"

Father hesitated for a moment, then answered, "I guess he

worked hard to make his millions. In America they are all self-made men.''

Mother persisted, "I know he is a self-made millionaire, but what has he done with his millions? Does he give any to the poor? What kind of person is he?''

Father chided her gently, "Frankly, Emma, you almost seem to be exhibiting a prejudice against millionaires!''

Mother laughed and said, "All right, we'll entertain him with dry biscuits and lemon tea!''

She served more, of course, but as far as she was concerned, Mr. Pierpont Morgan hadn't done anything too special for God or man. If he had, she didn't know anything about it. That was the only time I heard anyone in our family express anything like a prejudice.

On one occasion during my first year of lecturing in America I was in the South. My hostess' car was driven by a Negro chauffeur. He was so light-skinned that I didn't realize he was a Negro. When I got out of the car I said to him, "Thank you. You certainly did a very good job of driving in this dense traffic.'' He was visibly astonished and said, "Thank you, Miss.''

Afterwards my hostess reproached me, "We don't talk to our Negro chauffeurs, you know.'' Through incidents such as this I gradually became acquainted with racial prejudice.

On another occasion I was visiting a city in Louisiana or Tennessee where I was to give several lectures. My hostess was very interested in matching me up (I was single then) with a prominent lawyer who had political ambitions. At almost every opportunity she kept bringing us together. He was a nice-looking gentleman, but the way she spoke about her reasons for bringing us together had me stymied.

She said, "It's high time he was separated from his Negro mistress. He already has three children by her. It's time he got married. You could hardly make a better match, my dear.''

I looked at her and retorted, "You mean I'm supposed to take another woman's place?''

"Oh,'' she said, "Negroes don't count. They have no souls, you know.''

I jotted that one down for reference. It shocked me beyond all words—"no souls.'' I returned to New York and went to see several priests.

146

They all shrugged their shoulders and said, "You know how it is."

I said, "No, Father, I don't know how it is,"

They answered, "You better start getting Americanized."

So I went to Columbia University to study American history. The Negro wasn't mentioned at all. I asked the professors why.

"Oh, we don't study the Negro. We study American history."

"But," I said to them, "much of your history is based on slavery and plantations."

"That's not American history," they said, "that's slavery."

At that time, Columbia did not teach anything about the Negro. They said, "If you want to learn about the Negro you have to go to 125th Street. There's a Negro library there and they give courses once a week."

Little did I realize that 10 years later I would be living next door to that library.

With such experiences behind me, it's no wonder that when I arrived in Harlem I asked myself, "Where have I landed anyhow?" Father Mulvoy, our parish priest in Harlem, tried to explain things to me. He was a very holy man. He had organized many projects for his parishioners; he was very close to them and they loved him very much. But his explanations didn't satisfy me. I still felt I was in no-man's-land.

What astonished me most of all was that the Negroes accepted me because I was Russian. (They probably didn't know that Pushkin was the offspring of a Russian Princess and a Negro Prince. Even the Tsar attended their wedding.)

I began to help the Negroes as best I could, plunging into the interracial justice activities. I lectured on this subject all over the United States, but my soul was not at peace. I was facing an interior dilemma of fantastic proportions.

"In God We Trust" is printed on United States currency. But in travels to the small hamlets and large metropolises, minorities were disparaged with names like "Bohunks," "Polaks," "Kikes," "Dagoes," and the like. How could people call themselves Christians when they did not accept the Negro and the other minorities? This savored of an extreme type of racism.

One of the greatest pains I experienced was in relation to the church's attitude on this subject. I'm not speaking about the

Protestant churches, but about my own, although the other churches grieved me also by the way they treated the Negro. I began to have doubts.

Although my faith was strong, for maybe a year or so I underwent an agony, a temptation, that is very hard to describe. The temptation came from seeing the evil done by people in the U.S. to the Negro and the other minorities while mouthing the Gospel. This was hypocrisy. Where was God in it all? I used to spend nights praying on my linoleum floor in Harlem. Yes, Russia too was sinful. We had our pogroms. The Jews were the Tsar's scapegoats whenever anything went wrong. But these were nothing compared to what I saw in America.

When I came to Harlem I entered a no-man's-land of fear and doubt. It was the Christian, the Catholic, who was lying between the trenches, and he had to be rescued. I crawled into that no-man's-land where he was lying to drag him out and nurse him back to life. You know what? The "White Army" never stopped shooting! It wasn't like in the war. Oh no! Here, as you risked your life to save somebody, they kept on firing! I don't know how I survived. The hatred I saw in the people's faces when I lectured was enough to kill a hundred people.

At the request of the bishop I lectured once in Savannah, Georgia. (If you are going to preach the gospel with your life, you have to preach it everywhere. You can't say, "I'll preach it in New York but not in Georgia.) The southern "ladies" and "gentlemen" tore at my clothes until I was practically naked. My blouse was in shreds, and I was black and blue from the blows of the women.

At one point, as they were tearing off my skirt, a pair of Negro hands from behind the stage curtain grabbed me. A deep Negro voice said, "I have never seen such hatred for a person before." The Negroes whisked me off to a doctor who treated my bruises free of charge. These good people then gave me clothing and paid my fare back to New York. A Negro stewardess on a Pullman nursed me very kindly. I was half out of my mind. I had never experienced a mob of people trying to tear me apart!

At Friendship House in Harlem feelings had to be disregarded. You had to begin each day with faith. You knew that every day you would be attacked by someone.

A white man would walk in and spit in the middle of the

floor. "That's for you, nigger lover! You white, bloody nigger lover."

Two of our staff wanted to throw him out, but I said, "Let him alone. People spat on Christ. He's only spitting on the floor, not on us." So they let him alone.

I lectured to nuns and priests about accepting Negroes into their schools and colleges. I was a pioneer in that.

I remember in particular a very select Catholic school for girls.

After the lecture the sister superior said to me, "Here at Holyoke we have spent long years in establishing ourselves as an institution. You come here and want us to take in Negroes. It will ruin our whole image."

I was sitting across the table from her. I just stared at her and began to cry. I didn't say anything.

She asked, "Why are you crying?"

I said, "I am crying because a person like you who has dedicated herself to God, who is a bride of Christ, speaks the words of the devil."

I didn't stay too long afterward. They didn't even invite me to supper!

There were many, many instances like that. It was like a broken record. The superiors and the heads of the schools would always say, "How could we survive if we took in Negroes? We would lose all our students. It's impossible!"

One night in Harlem a rather stout, young, good-looking Negro came in. I knew her, she was a laundress. She said, "I want to talk to you."

"Sure," I said, "sit down."

She went straight to the point. "I have a problem. I go to St. Patrick's Cathedral. One Sunday morning the priest got up and said, 'You are going to hell if you don't send your children to a Catholic school. If you have any difficulty about it, see your parish priest or the bishop.'

"I said to myself, 'This is great. I live downtown and close to a Catholic school.' The next morning I went to the school and presented my two children for registration. The nun was a very severe-looking woman. She said, 'We don't take Negroes.' I answered, 'But Sister, the parish priest said to send our children to Catholic schools.' 'Go and talk to the parish priest,' she said.

"The parish priest said, 'No Negroes.' I went to the bishop. The bishop said to put my children in a Catholic school in Harlem. But that's 105th Street. I live below 42nd. It's impossible. We can't afford that."

She looked right at me and said, "What are you going to do about it?"

"I'm going to see the Cardinal," I answered.

After telling the Cardinal the whole story I asked, "How can you have interracial justice in your diocese if people get this kind of runaround from priests and nuns?"

He said, "Give me her address."

I gave him the address. The laundress came in to see him and told him the whole story. He called in the parish priest and the sister and asked for an explanation. There was none. The children were accepted into the school.

Incidents like this were common. A Negro woman became a convert to the Catholic Church through Friendship House. She was very excited and wanted to tell her friend all about it. She said, "My friend is still in the dark and is looking for some kind of church. I think I will take her to see the stations of the cross in a church in the Bronx. You know the ones I mean. They are very beautiful."

So they went to make these stations of the cross. They were all enthused. I remember giving them a little book to guide their devotion. As they were making these stations the parish priest came along and said, "No Negroes allowed." They were at the third or fourth station!

They immediately took a taxi and came to see me. I got a little hot under the collar. I had the private telephone number of Cardinal Hayes. He had given it to me because he was always worried about me. I called him, and he told me to take a taxi and bring them both over. My convert friend told him what had happened.

The Cardinal went right to the telephone and called the pastor. "Come right down here and apologize to these two women," he said. "I'm waiting for you."

The pastor came and apologized. I suspect there was a pastor in the Bronx who hated me!

It's hard to write about all this. It was really a martyrdom.

Night after night, day after day, my inner suffering was excruciating. Because I was suffering, I spoke passionately. I didn't hold in my pain in any way. It poured out and gave tremendous power to my words. Speaking was an outlet for this pent-up emotion. "Out of the depths I cry to you, O Lord. Lord, hear the voice of my supplication." No, I cannot adequately describe what I experienced in Harlem.

The Russians had said I was a courageous woman. As a nurse during the war they gave me the Medal of St. George, the highest award for bravery a nurse can receive. I've described the incident that led to that decoration. But who gives out decorations for standing still in the middle of hell in order to simply love people who have been innocently condemned to that hell?

I cannot describe the compassion, the fire of love that burned in my heart for those Negro people. It is impossible to put it down on paper. Harlem was a no-man's-land where, if you went out to rescue somebody, somebody else would shoot you down.

For example, the stories that followed me to Harlem were horrendous, although Archbishop McGuigan in Toronto wrote a beautiful letter to Cardinal Hayes in New York which said in effect, "Our loss is your gain."

But priests would come in and say, "They threw you out of Canada, didn't they? Well, of course, when you are thrown out of Canada, where else could you land but in Harlem!"

In Harlem I had a little room with a refrigerator, a tub for washing clothes and dishes, and a gas stove. It was a small room but it had everything I needed. I had a desk, a picture of St. Francis, a crucifix over my bed and a statue of our Lady. It was very humble.

My room in Harlem had the same kind of patched linoleum floor as my little room in Toronto. I used to lie on that linoleum and cry out to God: "Why have you brought me here? Why have you asked me to try to bring racial justice to a land born from a revolution for justice?" I couldn't understand all these contradictions. It was all mixed up. Truth and untruth—all mixed together. The United States had this marvelous Constitution, but it didn't apply to Negroes. "The pursuit of happiness!" For whom? Whites only.

When I first went to lecture on interracial justice, I wept. I cried to God, "This is impossible!" Priests warned me that this wasn't the time, that I was wrong, that I was going to hell, that mixing Negroes and whites would lead nowhere. If the priests were treating me like this, what could I expect from the laity?

Yet, always, the Spirit urged me on and gave me courage. You have to preach the gospel without compromise or shut up. One or the other. I tried to preach it without compromise.

I ended all my lectures this way: "Sooner or later, all of us are going to die. We will appear before God for judgment. The Lord will look at us and say, 'I was naked and you didn't clothe me. I was hungry and you didn't give me anything to eat. I was thirsty and you didn't give me a drink. I was sick and you didn't nurse me. I was in prison and you didn't come to visit me.' And we shall say, 'Lord, when did I not do these things?' " I would stop here, pause, and in a very loud voice say, *"When I was a Negro and you were a white American Catholic."* That was the end of the lecture. That's when the rotten eggs and tomatoes would start to fly!

I was a stranger in a strange land!

Then there was the wealth of the presbyteries where the priests lived. Once I talked to Cardinal Spellman about it. He said, "Catherine, I am a very lucky person. I have you and Dorothy Day praying before the face of the Lord, because your lives are a prayer. I am weak. Ask the Lord that I might always be on your side of the fence. I'll do everything I can. Whether you know it or not, a bishop is not always in complete control of his priests!"

Things were getting worse in the interracial field. (This was around 1940.) The Negroes were very restless. Cardinal Spellman, Bishop Sheil (James Sheil of Chicago) and Cardinal Stritch (Samuel Stritch of Chicago) decided that I had better visit the ordinaries of the Southern dioceses to warn them.

I was in a Southern town buying something in a five-and-ten, when suddenly I recognized the janitor.

"Heavens, what are you doing here?" I said. He was an Oxford graduate.

He said, "I'm doing on my side of the fence what you are doing on your side," and he kept sweeping.

He was a communist Negro, highly educated. When a white man came in my friend lifted his cap and said very loudly, "Yes, suh!"

152

Moving as I was among the Negroes, and hearing what they had to say, I could go to the bishop of any diocese in the South and tell him what was going on right under his nose. This is what I was commissioned to do. They paid my fare.

In New Orleans I hailed a taxi and asked for the Roman Catholic bishop's residence.

"Do you know where it is?" I asked the Negro driver.

"Oh yeh," he said, "the big shot with the fat belly that travels in a Rolls-Royce. Sure, we all know him."

I said, "Do you like him?"

He said, "That bastard! But, ha, I shouldn't be talking to you. You're white—but you don't look white to me. You have a funny accent."

I said, "I come from Russia."

He said, "Oh, Russia! Let's have a cup of coffee together."

All I had to do was say a few words in my thick Russian accent and I really got an earful.

I went all through the South like this—Alabama, Tennessee, Louisiana, Florida. It was wartime. Florida especially was a hotbed of communist activity. In San Francisco there were the Chinese, and the American government wondered if the yellow races would band togther. I helped to allay those fears. I was sort of on a secret mission, telling the bishops about the extent of communist infiltration among their people. It was frightening.

In Harlem itself a good many Negroes were becoming Catholics, and I soon discovered why. It was easier to get welfare that way, and the sisters were good to the children. When I saw what was happening I started classes for the new "converts." I asked the parish priests if I could invite their converts for a breakfast after their First Communion. At these breakfasts I would ask them, "Now that you've become Catholics, will you love the white people?" That stopped them cold. "Do you think the white people, the Catholics, will now love you because you have become Catholics? Will you now love your enemies? Have you really been converted to Jesus Christ?" It wasn't long before I was forbidden to have those breakfasts!

But we couldn't be stopped from organizing study groups. We called them liturgical or bible groups. I remember (God rest his soul) the pastor of St. Charles Borromeo Church. He walked in one night and said, "Listen to me, you Russian nitwit. What are you trying to do? Make them think they are loved just because they have become Catholics? You are giving them the raw gospel and it isn't getting you anywhere. Stop it!" I said, "Father, would you like to come with me to see the Cardinal? If he orders me to stop, I will stop." "Oh hell," he said. On the way out he slammed the door and smashed the glass in the window.

A stranger in a strange land!

The Jesuits at Fordham University in New York tried to convince me that they could not accept Negro students. Over a three-year period I had presented Fordham with a Negro candidate, a different young man each time. Each had a certificate from his parish priest attesting that he was a daily communicant, an ideal parishioner, that his high school average was over 90 percent and that he was a very good baseball, basketball or football player, whatever the case may have been. Each time the young man had been refused admission.

Once the Jesuits invited me to Fordham to lecture. They lined the gallery as I walked to the stage. The students filled the hall. I began: "I came to talk to you, not to lecture. In 10 minutes, therefore, I am stepping off this platform. Ten minutes is no lecture, as far as I am concerned. The situation here is very tragic. You have a chapel in this building, and there is a crucifix in the chapel. This same cross shines all over New York. However, the words of the person who died on that cross are ignored in these holy precincts."

I named one of the boys I had sent to them. "According to your teachers, the administration has turned thumbs down on his admittance here. They have told me that you do not want undergraduate Negroes. That's why I am getting off this platform right now."

It was a short, powerful speech, and the whole audience exploded. They surrounded the platform and shouted, "No, don't go. Talk to us! Talk to us!"

Well I started talking, and in my whole life I don't think I have ever given such a lecture on interracial justice as I gave that night. I put everything that was in me into it. When I finished, there was dead silence, I myself had gooseflesh.

Somebody quietly got up and said, "I'm asking for a show of hands. Are we accepting Negroes or not?"

There were unanimous cries of "Yes! Yes!"

I said, "Thank you. I am sure God is happy tonight."

The students were happy, God was happy, but the "Jebbies" were not happy. It was after this chain of events that I was invited to dinner and a private meeting.

The Jesuits asked a Mr. Callaghan, one of our volunteers and a graduate of Fordham, to take me to dinner. It was a "condemned man eat a hearty breakfast" state of affairs. You must admit, the Jesuits do things nicely. Callaghan, the poor man, was not too happy about his assignment.

"Ever since you lectured at Holyoke," he said, "the Jesuits have wanted to talk to you. So I have been delegated to invite you to dinner on their behalf."

I said, "Okay." (Dinner is always good!)

He took me in a cab to a swanky restaurant. I started with cocktails, followed by some vichyssoise. It couldn't have been better. Some red wine, and even champagne. To top it all off—cognac in the coffee!

I had foreseen what was about to happen, so I arrived with my little 25-cent Bible, the ribbons placed at appropriate texts. We sat in a very lovely living room. I sat in a leather chair facing Father Robert Gannon, the president of Fordham. There were about 20 other priests, all quite slender and good-looking, dressed in their nice cassocks and belts.

"Baroness," one of them began, "you realize, don't you, that many of our students are from the South. If we accept a Negro there will be a great hullabaloo among the parents and the students."

I said, "Oh, excuse me, Father, I thought you were teaching Christianity here." There was dead silence. I continued, "I have a little gospel book here. I would like to read something that I think fits this situation."

Nobody asked me to read it.

Another priest began: "Baroness, we have to move slowly. The time it not yet ripe."

I said , "Is that so, Father? I have never read anywhere in the gospel where Christ says to wait 20 years before living the gospel. The Good News is for *now*. He died for all men, to make all men his brothers and sisters, children of his Father. He didn't advocate brotherhood in 20 years or 100 years. He expects it to be now. He said, 'Go and preach the gospel,' and he means it. Have you ever read the gospel from that point of view, Father?"

It was someone else's turn. "But we will go broke!"

I said, "It's a question of what you're more interested in, God or mammon. God said you cannot serve two masters."

For almost two hours they badgered me with objections, and I refuted them as best I could. Their great temptation was to compromise with the gospel. The last sentence I remember saying was, "Fathers, please don't ask me over anymore. I love you very much. Your Founder has been a big influence in my own life. A Jesuit guided me spiritually when I was only 12 years old and living in Egypt. Don't break my heart. What you are doing is compromising with the gospel. Ignatius of Loyola would never do that."

I arose, bathed in perspiration. I have never gone through such a two-hour session in my life! I was being tested, but what could they say? I was living in Harlem, and I was trying to live the gospel without compromise. Really, what could they say?

A stranger in a strange land.

Over a period of years I was terribly perturbed by scenes like that. Priests were the men I loved most of all, next to God. I loved them almost more than I loved my own father and mother. They were the men I respected, no matter what they did. They were my fathers in Christ. They were supposed to lead me to God. Everything they said I took to heart.

After such sessions I used to return to my little room, lie down before the crucifix, and say, "Catherine, maybe you are misunderstanding the situation." I always wanted to give them the benefit of the doubt. But in the end I cried, because I knew I was right.

14. Identification with the Poor

When an apostolic group hits a place like Harlem, where the ordinary necessities of life are lacking, it is quite obvious it will direct its primary attention to fulfilling those needs. But it must be remembered that "Not by bread alone does man live." Friendship House Apostolate, and now Madonna House Apostolate, always tried to remember this most important truth. We performed works of mercy all day long.

It is difficult to describe this part of our apostolic work. How can one put these "intangibles" on paper? How is one to explain what we call the "chitchat" apostolate which was always part and parcel of our approach? It was another way of creating friendships—apparently very informal, but really not so.

Take, for instance, the simple act of walking half a block from my apartment on 138th Street to Lenox Avenue, then down three blocks on Lenox, then a half block on 135th Street to our library. Every day, with few exceptions, around 9:30 a.m. or so, I made that walk. One can make such a walk filled with one's own thoughts and problems, quite unconcerned about people along the way. Or, one can love, be aware of and concerned about everyone along the way.

I was not the only member of our staff who had to walk to the storefronts of Friendship House. Flewy (Grace Flewelling) walked from her room on 141st Street, a much longer walk than mine. Some of the staff workers lived in the Friendship House flat and only had to cross the street; others lived on 120th Street and on 139th Street.

Here is where I enter upon a description of these "intangibles," and I will speak only for myself. Other members of

157

Friendship House did what I did—perhaps in a different manner but with the same motivation and results. It was part of our way with the people.

All along my four blocks there were stores. When I walked by the store owners and their salesclerks were busy sweeping the sidewalks, washing windows, cleaning their stores, and getting ready for the day's work. I simply made it a point to stop at each place, or step inside if they were not working outside. At least I would stick my head through the door and bid them a cheery good morning and ask how business was doing.

As time went on, this led to longer conversations. At the corner of 138th Street and Lenox there was a Jewish pawnshop. The clerks were Negroes. I got to be quite friendly with everyone there. If I missed a day or two, due to a lecture tour or some other reason, they were concerned about me and very glad to see me back. Over a period of time I got to know all about the families of the clerks and the owners. We had most cordial relations and, if I may say so, even deeply friendly ones.

There was also a cleaning establishment; I used to take my clothes there. The girl who ran that establishment became a very dear friend. Though she was a Protestant, she attended our Lecture Forum and volunteered for some work on her free night. Another bridge of love had been established.

The grocery store, the wine merchant, and the barbershop were next in line. Here I established the same kind of relationships. The barber, years later, said he had become a Catholic just because of those little chitchats we had every morning. The manager of the beauty salon next to the barbershop also became a Catholic as a result of our morning visits. At the drugstore on the corner of 135th Street and Lenox I knew all the clerks intimately. They became deeply interested in the work of Friendship House.

There were no stores at all on the half block of 135th Street, but there were some brownstone fronts around which children played and women gossiped. On good warm days the women sat on kitchen chairs out front and visited with one another. Since it was a time of unemployment, men often joined them, or formed groups of their own.

Every day I went to each and every one of these people and wished them a good morning. If I didn't know them too well, I just nodded and smiled. Usually my progress down the street was slow, for I would stop at every little stairway of each brownstone. I spent a few moments visiting with the adults, and would also talk to the children who, for the most part, belonged to our youth club. This is why it took me almost three-quarters of an hour to make a trip of four blocks. Out of this chitchat apostolate, the identification with the people took place—always the hardest part of any apostolic work.

There was another form of our chitchat apostolate, a kind of suspension bridge at first, fragile and terrifying. Slowly, slowly it became a solid, well-built steel span of friendship. This was our delivery of clothing and other goods directly to families in need.

Let's say a mother came to our clothing room with a list of things for several of her children, and at the time we only had enough things for one or two. Knowing how difficult it was for her to leave her house, we promised to deliver the goods in person as soon as they arrived.

And so we would. In turn, many of us had very free access—not like social workers, but a more spontaneous access—to families. We would bring the parcel and they, in their tremendous hospitality (the poor are so hospitable!) would offer us a cup of coffee, which we would invariably accept.

How many realities of their lives were revealed to us over these cups of coffee! How much sorrow, pain, worry and even a few little joys were told to us in friendship over a kitchen table which often had a fourth leg propped up with bricks. Conversations like that are the essence of any life of love, and always will be. They were the core and essence of Friendship House, and they are of Madonna House today.

I have often spoken of identification with the poor. By that I mean an identification of love that is color-blind. It is an identification that only love can achieve by complete forgetfulness of self and total concern for the other person. It is an identification so deep, so complete, that it becomes part of oneself—like breathing! It is a way of love that is willing—nay, eager—to be a Simon of Cyrene to the passion of Christ in men. Not reluctantly, but eagerly and joyfully, this love picks up the cross carried by the neighbor—the heavy cross of pain, sorrow, and fear, and shares the weight of it as far as is humanly possible—and a little beyond!

This identification is a love that incarnates the abstract words we use so glibly every day—"sympathy," "empathy," "understanding." It makes them come alive under its touch. It is a personalized love that never counts the cost of giving.

This type of identification also entails a change of life-style: One must live like those with whom one wishes to identify. It would have been impossible to identify ourselves with the Negroes in Harlem *if we had not lived in Harlem.* We had to be poor as they were poor. We had to experience the way of life they experienced. We had to experience the crowded apartments with their poor ventilation; unbearably hot in the summer and unbearably cold in the winter. We had to experience the poor plumbing which, at times, could threaten our very lives.

I remember taking a bath once in Friendship House flat where the cold water tank was an old-fashioned contraption over a bathtub. Fortunately, I was standing up and soaping myself when this "contraption" broke loose and fell with a tremendous clamor, damaging both the tub and the floor. Had I been sitting in the tub, it would have hit me on the head and killed me for sure. One had to accept all these things—the bedbugs, the cockroaches, the noisy streets, the blaring radios that vied with one another day and night in making hideous noises.

Because we identified in these ways, those who received things from us did not hate us. They began to love us. The law of love, the law of Christ, began to work in Harlem in a tangible way. This was the cement of the whole structure of love, of the whole apostolate. Such cement is not easy to make. Its source is God, and prayer was the channel through which it came to us from him.

Every day at 7 a.m. we assisted at Mass together in our little church, St. Mark's, run by the Holy Ghost Fathers. I had breakfast in my "hermitage," and the staff ate in the Friendship House flat. After breakfast we came together. I had much work to do before this meeting. Before the work of the day we recited Prime together in the flat.

After our noon meal we went to St Mark's for spiritual reading. This might be done either privately or separately, depending on the calls of charity that day. Then we made a visit to the Blessed Sacrament and recited the rosary.

After supper, together with our volunteers (usually quite a

few), we recited Compline. Each one had his or her private prayers as well. Every year we made a three-day retreat. Every month we tried to have a day of recollection. We didn't always succeed in this, but we tried never to let it go beyond six weeks. In those days, we made our meditations in the privacy of our own rooms.

After we realized the tremendous pressures that a 6:30 a.m.-11 p.m. day could place upon our weary human shoulders, we arranged the schedule of the staff so that every six or seven weeks each person had a weekend in a monastery or convent. This was at the suggestion of our chaplain and our spiritual director.

Fortunately for us, New York and vicinity boasted of many such oases, so we had a wealth of choices. At the order of Cardinal Spellman, we inaugurated vacation—two weeks for the staff, and four weeks for local directors. We always begged our vacation money because the treasurer of Friendship House never would allow for such expenditures. Frequently we vacationed at Combermere in Ontario where my cousin Nicholas had built the framework of what is today Madonna House. Also, we tried to give each staff worker a half-day off every week. This didn't work out very well because the calls of charity were so numerous that these half-days were generally forgotten.

It is easy to describe these externals of our apostolate, but it is difficult to describe the intangibles that cemented that work into an edifice of love and grace. I have tried to do my best. It was the story of souls in travail, of pioneers in the unknown terrain of the lay apostolate. There is no denying that all of us, especially myself, travelled many a heavy and long "journey inward." Everyone in love with God must meet the Lord who dwells within his soul. All of us have to make that journey many times. I still do.

God blessed us with daily miracles in Harlem. One time, for example, I became very sick. The pain was intolerable. It centered around my ears which seemed to be on fire. My head also. It seemed to be terribly hot in my room, although it was cold outside. Strange to say, in that heat I felt cold, because I was thinking of the families who had so little coal.

The staff gave me some aspirin, and Flewy tried to give me something to drink. Then I heard her say, "Let's take her to the hospital, a Catholic hospital."

Somebody also said, "But she doesn't have any insurance, nor is she on welfare." I was thinking to myself, "Why are they all so worried about me? Why don't we simply pray to Jesus Christ?"

In my terrible pain and fever it was very clear to me: All I had to do was walk up to him and ask him to heal me. In my mind (strange as it is!) I did that very thing. It seemed to me (although Flewy later said I did none of these things) that I got out of bed and walked to some place that looked like Palestine. I met Jesus Christ and I said, "Please cure me because I just can't afford to be sick. There is too much to do."

In the meantime, the strangest thing happened.

There was a friend of ours, a Mr. Murray. (It turned out that he was a member of the Murray family of Barry's Bay, a town just a few miles from Combermere. Coincidences such as this have alway crisscrossed my life.) He was a sort of Fool for Christ. He walked around like Benedict Joseph Labre. He went from church to church. Now you would see him at Mass; now praying in a church during the day. At six o'clock he would come out and start rummaging through garbage cans to get some food. Nobody knew where he slept. People laughed at him, shrugged their shoulders and said, "Who can tell, maybe he is a saint." He started coming to Friendship House and teaching the men the 15 mysteries of the rosary. He recited it with them whether they wanted to or not. Many just kept on playing cards or checkers, paying scant attention to Mr. Murray. The following incident was told me by Flewy afterwards.

St. Teresa and St. Francis House were right next to each other. I was sleeping upstairs in St. Teresa's. In St. Francis the men were sitting around as usual when this Mr. Murray walked in.

He said, "Where's Catherine?"

Flewy said, "She's terribly sick. She is going to be operated on tomorrow. She has abscesses in both ears."

He looked at her and said, "Nonsense, she doesn't have to be operated on. She has to serve the Lord." He started his 15 decades—and this time everybody joined him. Some of the men just bowed their heads, but nobody continued to play checkers.

When he finished, he announced, "She is not going to be operated on, that's for sure." He departed.

Flewy, much perturbed, came over to St. Teresa's and found

me sleeping quite peacefully and quietly for the first time in days.

The next morning I had no temperature. The doctor who came to see me had arranged for an ambulance.

Flewy said, "You had better come upstairs because something has happened."

He couldn't believe it! There were no abscesses whatsoever! By four o'clock that afternoon I was up and about and even went downstairs.

Who walks in but Mr. Murray, who simply remarked, "I said she had to serve the Lord."

Then he started his 15 decades of the rosary again!

Another time there was a flu epidemic. I came down with a temperature of 104°. They took me to the Harlem hospital where, according to Flewy, I was put on a bench somewhere until the doctors came. When they discovered that I had no insurance, was not on welfare, and was unemployed, they said good-bye. They told Flewy to take me back home and to contact the Welfare Department. Flewy took me back home in a taxi.

Flewy had to look after Friendship House, so some uneducated Negro woman nursed me. One very old woman wanted me to eat an egg. I had strep throat, and in those days there were no antibiotics.

She said, "What you need is an egg. It will go down nice and easy."

But we had no money to buy an egg.

Just as in my last illness I told Jesus that we had no money to go to the hospital, so now I said to him, "Eggs are expensive." But somebody went out and begged two eggs. So I had two eggs. In those days that was a luxury.

Then this old woman said, "Chile, you are mighty sick, mighty sick." A Negro doctor came twice and did what he could, but what could he do? Then the old woman said, "Chile, you are mighty sick. I am going to bring you a healer."

So she brought a Negro Pentecostal woman. This woman came in and put my head on her knee. I fell asleep, and the next morning I was better! Now what do you think about that!

There was terrible poverty in Harlem. Who can describe it! Everything was too expensive. We in Friendship House had money, often thousands of dollars, passing through our hands. I

163

wasn't very good at banking it because the needs around us were so great.

If I was given a hundred dollars one minute, the next minute a woman might walk in and say, "I need an operation. I have the insurance for the hospital but the doctor says he has to pay the anesthetist a hundred dollars. The doctor is willing to do my operation for nothing, but the anesthetist isn't. Where can I get a hundred dollars?" I would give her the hundred dollars. Money went so quickly like that, so quickly.

I tried to give our staff a balanced diet, although during wartime food was rationed. We had prunes every morning, porridge (which was very cheap in those days), and corn flakes. We rarely had milk, but you can learn to drink coffee and eat cereal without it. The meal was sufficient and filled the stomach.

At noon there was the eternal soup. Donated food went into it, and many people came to share it. Flewy used to say, "I wish I had enough soup. It is good and thick but there is never enough." We served bread with the soup, then prunes again for dessert. For supper, soup again, or beans.

We served these meals in our little apartment across from the library. People were "converted" while eating. Even big shots came once or twice a week to eat with us. One person said, "This is monotonous, excruciatingly monotonous." I answered,"Yes, it is, but that's how the poor eat. We eat like they do."

Cardinal Spellman arrived one day when we were having stew. He said, "Catherine, your food is a little better than the Catholic Worker's, but not much!" Nobody said anything. He couldn't find any meat. (Even if a little meat came in on Fridays and Wednesday's during Lent, we didn't eat it.) He looked around and asked, "By any chance, are you observing the fasting regulations?"

Everybody smiled a big smile and answered, "Of course, Your Eminence. We are fasting for many intentions—the poor, the Negro, peace."

"Well," he said, "your Father doesn't want you to fast. If you get a piece of meat, you go right ahead and eat it on any day of the week. But don't forget to pray for me." So we were dispensed from abstinence. The funny part was, we never received much meat anyhow, but we didn't tell him that!

One day a Russian refugee from Canada came in. Kossoff was tall and very handsome, a Rudolph Valentino type, with a beard and all.

He said to me, "Catherine, I haven't any money."

I answered, "Neither have I."

He said, "How would you like to dance the tango with me and make some money?"

I said, "Sure, let's try."

We went to Greenwich Village.

I wore an evening gown and he wore a tuxedo. We started dancing together in a cocktail lounge and were quite successful. A collection was taken up afterwards and we made 10 dollars. My God that was a lot of money! So we went into this dance routine in a big way and started to become quite popular.

Nobody "booked" us, but if I passed by a cocktail lounge during the day, the manager might say, "How about coming tonight with your boyfriend?" (He wasn't my boyfriend.)

We made the circuit of the bars in Greenwich Village and always split the take fifty-fifty.

Kossoff was an artist, and his ambition was to work in Hollywood. One day he received a telegram offering him a job at the Walt Disney Studios.

He drew cartoons, and several years later married a very rich woman. I lost sight of him after that.

During our dancing days, a young man kind of attached himself to me. He introduced himself as Mr. Wright. This didn't mean anything to me. He asked me once, "Would you like to come and meet my father?" Do you know who his father was? The architect, Frank Lloyd Wright!

There were some very sad moments in my life. Once I was invited to the Catholic Daughters of America to give a lecture on interracial justice. Coffee and tea were served after the lecture. A lady poured my tea, then set it down on the edge of the table and said, "I prefer that you take it yourself. You must be dirty since you eat with dirty niggers." I took the cup. There were some oohs and aahs, but I didn't say anything, just turned around and started talking to somebody else. When I returned home I told the story to the staff.

Several weeks later we went with our boys and girls to a basketball game. On the way home we passed the cocktail lounges. Many rich people were out slumming. Suddenly, a white lady came out of one of the lounges hanging on the arm of a very tall and handsome Negro. He turned around and kissed her on the lips. As her face lifted, I recognized her and she recognized me. It was the lady who wouldn't pass me the cup of coffee at the Catholic Daughters of America lecture.

A half hour after I arrived home the phone rang. It was this lady and she was crying. I said to her, "Relax, I didn't see anything." She was very grateful. Incidentally, her daughter attended Manhattanville College and periodically came to help us, though her mother, the wife of a prominent New York doctor, was not aware of this.

When in Harlem I often dreamt of being black. That's why John Howard Griffin's book *Black Like Me* gripped me so much. I read and reread it many times. He had embodied my dream. It was such a pain to me that I couldn't become black.

It was dangerous to walk with black people, especially with a black man, outside of 105th Street. Betty Schneider, one of our staff, was taking some black kids swimming. The kids were ahead, and Betty was walking with a young Negro man when some white men jumped them. They beat them up and left them lying bloody in the street. That's the way it was living in Harlem in those days.

To live among the Negroes in those days was to live among the pariahs of society. When we walked into a room people would often say, "You smell of the Negro." Usually I passed them by without saying anything. But I must admit, once in a while I would retort, "And you stink of hell!" But I didn't do that too often!

To lecture about the Negro was to take your life in your hands.

Once I lectured in Flatbush. Do you know what was thrown at me there? A cabbage! Have you ever been hit by a cabbage? It struck me right on the temple, and I fell down. You could call me a confessor of the faith struck down by a cabbage! Some people are wounded with knives. Others are pelted with stones or with something equally exciting. Me, I get hit with a cabbage!

Living in Harlem was both heaven and hell. The hell had been created by men, the heaven by God. Even to this day, my heart smiles at the sight of a Negro face, because to me it is like an icon of Christ. I was so at home in Harlem, so at home.

166

I knew I would eventually leave Harlem, But I didn't know the separation would come the way it did. I cannot describe what happened to me when I left Harlem. I wasn't really thrown out. I could have easily thrown out those who wanted to get rid of me because I had the support of the church authorities.

But what can you do against an "Order in Council?" You can't do anything. They wanted to have a different kind of Friendship House, not the one that God had put into my heart. They wanted the one that was in their hearts. I couldn't fight that, could I? Not very well. So eventually I left.

I was part of two Harlems—the Harlem of daily existence and the Harlem that broke my heart—again and again. But there were many, many good things that happened in Harlem. Eddie Doherty happened.

One day the door of the library opened and a man and woman walked in. He was good-looking, somewhat graying and sported a military moustache. Without a moment's hesitation he walked up to me and introduced himself: "I am Eddie Doherty of *Liberty* magazine, and this is my assistant."

I wasn't exactly a fan of *Liberty*. In fact, at one time I had put it on the censored list for my son, not because it was bad, but because it was too light. I said, "What can I do for you, Mr Newspaperman from *Liberty*?" He said, "We have an assignment, my friend and I, to write about the wickedest city in the world—Harlem."

I exploded! "Is that right! Would you ever consider writing about something else, like exactly *why* this is the wickedest city in the world?"

He parried: "Why *is* it?"

This was my first dialogue with Mr. Doherty. I answered, "*You* made it so."

He said, "I made it so?"

I said, "Yes, all of you white Americans. It wouldn't be the wickedest city if everybody could get out of Harlem and live anywhere they wanted to. Okay? So I don't see what I can do to help you write such damn nonsense as you want to write."

He pointed to his companion. "This lady tells me that you are the only person who really knows Harlem. She says you are a baroness living in Harlem for the love of God. I am interested in

167

the fact that you really know Harlem inside out. I want to get the real picture of Harlem."

I said, "Well, you can go right out the door because I am not telling you anything about Harlem, that's all there is to it." I added, "Why don't you write an article, 'Harlem, the Saintliest City in the World'? After all, these people are under your heel and still they survive, they pray, and they go to church. I don't see any reason for writing the kind of article you have in mind."

Much later I discovered that this was Eddie's technique, his way of getting information. He annoyed people, made them angry, and then they talked. It certainly worked: I was very annoyed. He said, "I'll come back again. I understand that you are doing very good work here. May I make an offering?" He put a check for $400 in my hand.

I said, "Look, I've been in the newspaper business myself. You guys don't have that kind of money. You either drink it up or simply don't have any. So why do you want to show off and have your check bounce?"

The girl came to his rescue, "Oh, no! He's not that kind of person. He is the highest paid reporter in America."

I said, "All right, I'll take the check, but I just hope it doesn't bounce."

They both left. From then on Edward J. Doherty became a frequent visitor to Friendship House. He seemed to be very interested in one of our staff; she was certainly interested in him. A whole group of girls seemed to be attracted to him, but I wasn't particularly.

Eddie kept coming back, always under the guise of wishing to learn more about Harlem. One day he said, "You know something? I'd like to write your story." I said, "For Pete's sake! My story!" He began to take me out evenings, to Third Avenue, or to a Negro bar where I liked to hear the Negro bands. He sort of attached himself to me, and people joked about it; but I never paid much attention to the whole deal.

Today, as I look back, I see that he acquired all his information for *Tumbleweed* (his biography of me) from those evening conversations. He would ask, "So your father even went to Egypt, did he? And to Japan? And China, too? You certainly were a well-traveled girl from a very early age." His questions brought back memories of father and mother. I had never talked to anybody

168

about them, and it was very pleasant to do so.

He was very delicate in asking about the Baron. "Does your son look like your husband?" Yes, he was very smooth. I never "tumbled" to the fact that he was a writer acquiring information. No, he never mentioned that once.

After a while he suddenly stopped taking me out so often. Then one day he appeared and said, "Catherine, I have written a book about my conversion after the death of my second wife. Father Charles Coughlin really forced the issue for me. I wrote it up in *Liberty* as 'No Soul No Story.' "

That caught my interest.

He continued, "This book in my autobiography. I'm not too familiar with Catholic publishers. Would you mind trying to sell it for me?"

He was, of course, very familiar with Catholic publishers. This whole speech was merely a come-on. He added, "I'll give you a little percentage." Well, I spent the whole night reading that book, it was so fascinating and so interesting. I began to see Eddie Doherty in an entirely different light. *That*, of course, is what he had hoped would happen.

What I read was *Gall and Honey* in manuscript form. I said later, "Selling that story will be no problem." Sheed and Ward bought it right away. Only then did it dawn on me that he could have sold it anywhere, anytime, but he wanted me to read it so that my attitude toward him would change. It worked magnificently! My attitude did change. I saw a gentleman, a fighter, a man of the people, a lace-curtain Irishman. I sensed his goodness. It came through in his words. From that day on I began to be really interested in him, very interested.

He had a marvelous car which was the joy of all the Harlem kids. Ellen Tarry, one of the staff workers, wrote a book about it: *The Red Car*. It had a special horn that played (I think) "When Irish Eyes Are Smiling"! To put the top up when it rained, all you had to do was press a button. It had a radio and just about everything a car could have in those days.

He was a sharp dresser, too—Donegal Tweeds and all the rest!

One day he invited me to his house, a 10-room residence in Larchmont, Westchester County. He lived there with his two sons. One was away at school at this time, and the other lived at home.

His wife had organized the house, and it was very well furnished. There was a lovely garden as well. There was a housekeeper. I finally realized that he was indeed very rich, receiving a fabulous salary from *Liberty*.

On another occasion, while traveling in Chicago, we stopped at a place called "The Kennels." Suddenly he took me in his arms and kissed me. He said, "Don't you know I am in love with you? You can't deny that you are in love with me." I couldn't. I said, "Eddie, this is getting us nowhere," and kissed him back. But I realized that if he married me he would have to give up his whole life—his job, his house, his car.

By this time I was with a Friendship House in Chicago and we decided not to see each other again. We said good-bye in a park by Lake Michigan. It was the end—so I thought. He went to Hollywood to write the screenplay for *The Sullivan Brothers*.

When he returned he visited me and said, "Catherine, I want you to come with me to see Bishop Sheil." So we went to see the Bishop, and Eddie proposed to me right in front of the Bishop!

The Bishop said, "Eddie, you cannot marry Catherine because you are well-off, you have a high-paying job. If you want to marry her, Friendship House must come first." Eddie answered, "I will give it all up for her sake, because I love her."

"All right," said the Bishop, "kneel down, kiss my cross, and repeat after me that Friendship House will always come first, and you second. You can continue to write. But she lives as a beggar, so you will have to give away your money." Eddie agreed to all this, and a date was set for the wedding.

What Eddie was doing seemed absolutely terrible to me. He was making tremendous sacrifices, especially in giving up his newspaper work. However, we were finally married on June 25, 1943. The ceremony took place in the Bishop's Chapel, St. Andrew's Parish, Chicago. The Bishop wore, especially for the occasion, a vestment that had belonged to Saint Pius X. Eddie's whole family attended. I didn't invite anybody from Friendship House—didn't tell anybody from Friendship House about the wedding—because I didn't know what the reactions would be. I must admit I was frightened about that.

The Bishop had arranged everything for the wedding. For the wedding breakfast we had lobster with all the trimmings. The

170

Bishop had even arranged a hotel suite for us. It was, of course, wartime.

When we arrived at our suite a Marine, a friend of Eddie's family, was waiting for us! He had dinner with us, but then *finally* departed. Our honeymoon lasted three days.

Then I went to Friendship House and told them I was married. The shock was terrible! But since I wasn't under any vows as a lay apostle, and since my childbearing days were over, and especially because Eddie was going to give up everything for the apostolate, they accepted it.

Eddie and I lived in a little apartment in Chicago. It had a very tiny bath and kitchen, and a sort of living room with a Murphy bed and an alcove where Eddie could type. The house itself had quite a history. It had originally been the Addams House, the first settlement house in America. Dorothy Day's group had occupied it at one time also.

Because of my marriage to Eddie, a change was taking place which I didn't immediately understand. Because Eddie was Irish the priests changed tremendously in their attitude toward me. They still weren't sure about me, but now they were more careful! Behind me now stood a Doherty, and I began to understand. Many of the priests were Irish, Eddie was Irish. The non-Irish priests, of course, didn't have this same caution, but the Irish priests were careful. Since the majority of the priests were Irish, my lot in life improved in a very pleasant way!

Eddie abided by everything he had promised. When I would announce that I had to go lecturing in New York or some other place, all he would say was, "We'll have lunch at the station." He accepted my responsibilities for the apostolate without question.

There was about him such an incredible gentleness that at first I could not quite understand it. No one (except my parents) had ever been that gentle with me. Throughout the rest of my life, no one has ever treated me as gently as he did. It was so strange! Even in his lovemaking he was gentle, and it was very beautiful.

We always ended our lovemaking with Holy Communion. We would go together in the morning. I began to feel the fullness of marriage in the sense that we really were one in Christ. Truly it was a wonderful realization.

In 32 years of marriage Eddie and I had only one tiff. His ability to understand me was so strange and foreign to me. I guess the answer is simply that he loved me. When he had serious heart trouble in his later years, I found it very difficult, because then I couldn't talk to him as often. Whenever I talked to him he was able to smooth the way for me.

In 1946 the staff of Friendship House rejected me and my ideas. Eddie listened to everything that was said but never once opened his lips. At night he consoled me. I wonder if I could have gotten through 1946 without Eddie. He had promised to make me happy, and he did. Into the very midst of this tragedy and crucifixion came this man who brought me love, gentleness, understanding, and consolation.

When we finally left the United States for Canada in 1947, I was really bushed. It was the time of my first heart attack. I didn't pay much attention to it but tried to do the right things—scrub floors, walk, keep busy. Eddie made it easy.

Bishop Sheil gave us a car for the trip. We put about a hundred books in the back of the car and some luggage. We went to visit George who was graduating that day from Queen's University. We arrived in Combermere on May 17, 1947, leaving Friendship House and everything else behind.

However, there is no denying that I was sick in both heart and mind. During the early days in Combermere I was afraid of people, even finding it difficult to walk across the road to visit. I cured myself by saying, "This is what God wants us to do, be with people," and by organizing our new life in Combermere.

That's the story of my marriage, a joyous event that began in Harlem. Living in Harlem was like living in heaven in hell, if I can put it that way. It was also like dying. But this death was both very painful and exceedingly sweet. These paradoxes were the strange part of it all.

As we drove in Bishop Sheil's car toward Combermere on that day in May, 1947, I remember experiencing a fantastic sweetness. I can still taste it. It was as if God had kissed me, and his face was black.

15. Early Days in Combermere

May 17, 1947, was sunny and very warm. We stopped in Bancroft for a cup of tea and some cinnamon toast. Combermere and environs did not have the wonderful highways then which you see now. The road from Bancroft to Combermere was more like a secondary highway—narrow, twisting, scenic but dangerous. We didn't drive fast but took our time, filling our eyes with the beauty of the land. I acted as guide, telling Eddie what I knew about the country. My cousin Nicholas and I had spent many weeks here during the 30s, fishing and hiking.

We arrived around three o'clock in the afternoon. The first sight of the little, unfinished six-room house was exhilarating. Though it had no siding, and was unpainted, it still looked cozy. The statue of Our Lady of Guadalupe, which had been enshrined the year before, stood over the window of an upstairs room. We could see it from the road and it welcomed us.

The yard was just sand and weeds. Some wheat and oats from the old days were growing, and the grass was high and tough. There were hundreds of raspberry bushes, and wild strawberries everywhere. The front "lawn" was all sand. The beach extended to the front steps of the house, and there was no terracing of any kind.

We were hungry and tired. The little kitchen was cozy and clean. I had written one of the neighbors and asked her to clean the house for our arrival. She had washed the windows and stocked the pantry and icebox. We ate in the living room. In a state of great content, Eddie stared out at the Madawaska River and said, "Katie, welcome to your new home."

Three dozen young apple trees had been delivered a few days before our arrival. The field for the orchard had been ploughed and manured. All we needed now was a hole in the ground for each tree—and someone to dig it.

We unpacked and brought all the things into the living room. Since we had plenty of daylight left, I suggested that we plant our apple trees. I crossed the road and asked Desire Mayhew and Wilfred Bouchard, our immediate neighbors, if they would help us. In a very neighborly gesture they helped Eddie and me plant the 36 trees. These neighbors of ours dug the holes very quickly. Eddie got tired just watching them. We were finished by seven o'clock. Thus the orchard, in a sense, is a memorial. It was planted on the day we arrived, May 17, 1947, the Foundation Day of Madonna House.

Flewy, who had decided to come with us, was spending a few weeks in New York and Toronto first. In those weeks Eddie and I enjoyed a little privacy. This was helpful, because I began to suffer from the shakes, another delayed psychological reaction to the shock of leaving. They didn't last too long, but they came on several times a day. I tried to hide them from Eddie, but without success. Newspapermen have keen eyes. But in spite of the shakes and occasional tearful moments, I occupied myself with the obvious needs of Madonna House.

We didn't have much money, and purchases had to be made well ahead of time in these rural areas. Transportation was slow and uncertain. There was Lou Waddington's general store, Fitzgerald's meat market, and a post office in town. For something like ice cream you had to drive 10 miles to Barry's Bay. There was no electricity.

Madonna House was heated by a wood furnace (which we still use). We had a fireplace in the living room, and we had a kitchen stove. Our first purchase was wood. The price was only four dollars a cord, but we needed eight to ten cords a year. That put a big hole into our small supply of cash.

Although we were careful about the food budget I had to begin begging again. Now there could be no face-to-face begging from city friends, no begging by telephone or by personal invitations. We had to beg by mail—a very slow-motion affair, especially in the beginning.

We built an outdoor toilet. There was a hand pump in the

house and a well in the cellar. But it took a thousand strokes of the pump handle to fill the water tank! We made a study and discovered that we had to fill the tank at least three times a day to supply the water for cooking and laundry. That meant 3,000 times! When Flewy arrived we did the laundry in the river, as primitive peoples do. That reduced our pumping a little. Eventually, with money begged or borrowed, we installed an outdoor pump which was easier to manage. We then carried water in pails to the kitchen.

I bought 20 bags of potatoes and stored them for use during the long winter months. We also bought coffee, tea, butter, and flour. I baked my own bread, because it was much cheaper than any bread we could buy. I obtained milk from Mrs. Mayhew for 10 cents a quart, the prevalent price in 1947. I bought eggs from friendly farmers at 25 cents a dozen. All the same, we didn't eat many eggs.

Settling down, getting acquainted, and arranging for necessities kept me busy. I wanted greens during the winter so I lost no time in starting a garden. I planted radishes, beans, peas, Swiss chard, corn, and squash. In those days there were no stores which sold fresh vegetables, so our garden helped us very much. I think I also planted cucumbers and made pickles in the fall.

I did the washing, the mending, and the sewing. I wanted to take only the minimum from Friendship House, so we didn't have many clothes when we arrived in Combermere. I had brought some pieces of material that nobody wanted and did some sewing.

It was a rugged change from the big cities of Chicago and New York to the primitive, rural simplicity of Combermere, Ontario.

Soon after our arrival I organized what we now call the "master files." I had kept the Canadian addresses in the archives and had brought some American ones with me. When Flewy arrived we worked on these things together.

After getting the files in order, my next job was sending out a begging letter. By September, 1947, I had collected three or four hundred dollars, maybe a little more. I hired Ed Marquardt to put siding on the house. This made it much warmer. I had no more money, so the house remained unpainted.

One thing I must mention again: It was a traumatic shock for me to leave the premises of Madonna House. Strange as it may seem, I was afraid of people, afraid they would hurt me. I literally *made myself* go out with Flewy, or by myself, on the chitchat apostolate. That was the beginning of our new apostolate of Madonna House.

Let me give you the schedule of an average day during these early months—a day in summer and fall, and a day in the winter.

We rose at 5:30 a.m. because I had to start the bread. Flewy or I would start the wood stove in the kitchen (our only cooking stove, winter or summer), put the kettle on and cook porridge. Flewy usually took care of these chores three times a week. On the other days she cleaned the downstairs rooms. By 6:30 we were usually finished.

Then I woke Eddie and we went to Mass, if there was Mass. Father Pat Dwyer, the pastor of our little parish in Combermere, was a sick man, and he wasn't always able to celebrate Mass. If Father was on time, we said Prime after Mass. If he was delayed, we said it before Mass. The altar boys spread the story that when Father Dwyer was late, we said the Mass for him in the pews! We killed that story, but it took us quite a while.

Often the altar boys served Mass barefooted. It was a lovely old church, so suitable to our backbush country. At times we felt we were living in early Christian surroundings.

After Mass and Prime we returned home and had breakfast. We started our porridge in a double boiler before we left. We had banked the fire well so that it was nice and hot when we arrived. The stove was hot, the kettle was boiling. We made good strong tea and toasted bread over the flames of the stove. No toast ever tasted quite so good!

Breakfast over, I went into the flower garden. Even during that first May I started one. I was successful in growing ordinary annuals—zinnias, petunias, etc. I gave some to Father Dwyer for his altar. The local people would never use wild flowers for the altar. They did not consider them suitable for God. They preferred growing their own flowers for the church.

Hoeing, planting and watering were time-consuming chores. On Mondays I did the laundry, either on the boards or in the river. Most days I was busy in the morning with what could be called the outside chores. Eddie's job was to bring in the wood for the day from the woodpile outside. We had no woodshed.

About 11:30 a.m. I would be back in the kitchen. Usually a half-hour sufficed for me to make a meal. I am a fast cook. (The "half-hour" is not quite correct, because I used to boil things the night before—potatoes, carrots, and whatever vegetables I had on hand. They were then all ready for the mixes, stews, and "gooks" for which I was famous.)

We were poor, so, for two or three months, my cooking was easy. I served potatoes every which way—potato soup, potato pancakes, etc. Dinner over, Flewy and I walked to the church again—rain or shine—and made our visit to the Blessed Sacrament. We spent at least 10 minutes in spiritual reading aloud, and 20 minutes to ourselves. Then we returned home.

In the afternoon we wrote letters, organized the master files, sorted things in the archives and put our library in order. I had brought about a hundred books from Chicago, and there were some in the house. That was the nucleus for both our reference library and our lending library.

Around 4 p.m. we had a tea break, then Flewy went off to visit the neighbors, always widening her circle of friends.

I cooked supper, so I was always the first one home. It was my job, or Eddie's, to pick up the mail at the post office. It was located about a mile away, a nice walk in the summer. Often I used my bicycle to do my shopping and my chitchat apostolate. But as parcels began to arrive, the donations of clothing and goods for which I had begged, I used the go-cart. Due to the price of gasoline, we had to use the car sparingly.

Supper was even simpler than dinner. We did not hurry eating. We took time to discuss all that had happened during the day, and made plans for the following day. After dishes, Flewy, Eddie, and I recited Compline and the rosary. Eddie didn't always participate in our exercises; he had his own Dominican Office to say, and several rosaries.

In the evening I wrote more letters and worked on the files. I also cut out items of interest for future files and for future staff workers. In my begging letters, I had asked for magazines, both secular and religious. I cut out items for the benefit of future students of handicrafts, for those who would be working in the kitchen or the garden, for those who might be interested in beekeeping, or farming, or nursing.

My clipping was Flewy's pet peeve. Since we had no filing

cabinets, I used cardboard boxes with suitable folders. These cartons seemed to multiply (for I did extensive clipping!). Storage space was limited, so we were constantly moving these primitive file boxes from one place to another, from basement to attic and back again. Flewy could not see why I was always cutting out things which had no relation to what we were presently doing. I kept telling her, "Wait and see."

Every day Flewy cleaned the oil lamps and filled them. We began with about six lamps, but as our needs grew we ended up with about 15. It took an hour to clean, trim, and fill them.

During the summer months we bathed in the river and shampooed our hair. I used to go for a dip every morning, and then again at teatime. To take a bath when the weather was too cold to go in the river was quite an ordeal. There was no plumbing connected to the basement furnace or the kitchen stove. The hot water tank was heated by a tiny stove. We chopped wood and fed it to that little stove for two and a half hours to warm up a tank of water which only filled a quarter of the bathtub.

Flewy usually retired about eleven, but I often stayed up later to catch up on correspondence or a few office chores. Eddie spent most of his time writing books. At this time he was writing *My Hay Ain't In*, and a book about Fatima. This is the period when he suffered a heart attack.

On Sundays we went to Mass and continued getting acquainted with the neighbors on the front steps of the parish church. We also participated (for the same reason) in all the bazaars and picnics of the parish, working as waitresses, cooks, and dishwashers. Occasionally on Sundays we invited our neighbors over for tea, or went to visit them.

During September I had begged enough clothing to organize a "clothing room" in the cellar. It was a tight fit! Our laundry tubs, water system, and foodstuffs were also down there. But with a few shelves and hangers, I managed. Flewy let it be known quietly that if anybody was in need of clothing, it was available.

Slowly, people started coming. Soon, several a day. Some of them I knew. You must remember, I had been coming to Combermere every year or so since the early 30s. During the Depression I had sent hundreds of pounds of clothing from Ottawa's Friendship House to be distributed to the people of Combermere. They suffered from lack of clothing more than from lack of food.

Farmers manage to eat even during a depression.

After giving out clothing, it was my custom to offer a cup of tea to those who came. We would visit. Warmed by the tea, and I hope by charity (the love in my heart), they would tell me many of their troubles. We became more and more friendly. Flewy and I took turns serving in this clothing room.

Our six-room house, which seemed to us a quite ordinary place, was known to our neighbors as "the mansion." That was unfortunate because it was our desire to identify with the poor. God took care of that in due time.

By the end of September and the beginning of October, cold weather began. November brought the first snowfall. The garden chores were over and the wood chores started. This is where Eddie acquired his first real taste of rural living.

On some nights as much as a foot of snow accumulated on our woodpile. Eddie had to take a broom, sweep the snow off the pile, then take an axe and separate the pieces which were frozen together. If there was even a wee bit of sunshine during the day, the snow thawed, then froze during the night. After separating the logs, Eddie carried armfuls to the kitchen and stood them up like soldiers to dry out. It took longer to get the fire going in the wintertime.

One thing really depressed us—pumping water! But by October I had acquired enough money to make a down payment on a gasoline pump. Mr. Baily Adrain, a plumber and mechanic in Combermere, connected it for us. I cannot describe the terrific joy and excitement of having this gasoline pump! Even though it too demanded a lot of work, it sure beat pumping!

First of all, I had to fill it with a mixture of gasoline and oil. Then I had to prime it, which meant stamping a pedal with my foot until the spark caught. If the engine was cold, this could take a long time. (This is why my right thigh is more developed than my left.) Yet, it was much easier than pumping several thousand times a day by hand!

Another important purchase was a sewing machine. The T. Eaton Company accepted a down payment. Before this I had been doing all the mending by hand. Now I could do much more. I kept this machine in our bedroom. We were happy with these two new additions.

During the winter we were all "pathologists." A "pathologist," according to Eddie, was somebody who made paths after the heavy snowfalls!

Going to the post office during the winter was an ordeal. I couldn't use my bicycle; we very rarely took the car out at all. So we walked to the post office, no matter how much snow there was. Flewy developed varicose veins which impeded her progress.

We used a toboggan to bring back all the parcels that kept increasing in response to my begging letters. I used to make a special plea for Christmas cheer. There were so many poor families in Combermere who could use it. Once in a while, I would get a ride from a farmer who had come to town with his team of horses.

One of the most pleasant aspects of going to the post office was that I became well acquainted with Mr. and Mrs. Ralph Jenkins. Every day after picking up the mail I used to stop for a few minutes at their house and be offered a nice cup of tea to warm the cockles of my heart. I also visited daily with Mrs. Hudson.

Such were the early days of Combermere. People started coming from near and far. Some joined us, and Madonna House developed into a training center for the lay apostolate. Over the years thousands have found here hope and understanding, and even God, to whom be praise, honor and glory forever and ever!

Now I would like to say something of the deeper significance of Combermere, and speak about an accent to my vocation which I have not revealed before in my writings. To do this, I must speak again about my parents.

Grace builds on nature, and grace worked powerfully in my life through my parents. Their influence permeated and filled my life far beyond my 15th year. I have told so many stories about them to show how deeply Christian they were, and how my formation fell into their Christianity like a baby into a warm bath. I do not want to be repetitive, but I think it is imperative to tell stories about my parents so you can understand my own life.

During the year preceding my visit to the Ordinary of Toronto, to ask him about my vocation, I was tremendously drawn to the reading of the scriptures, especially the New Testament. My mind constantly dwelt in Nazareth. It seemed to me that what God was calling me to do—sell all I possessed, take up my cross and follow him into the slums—was actually to go to *Nazareth*.

The Eastern mind, or perhaps I should say the Russian mind, pictures Nazareth as the home of a simple workingman, his wife and Son. It marvels at the abasement of Christ the King, Lord of all creation, not only in becoming man, but in choosing the state of a worker-peasant who barely keeps his head above financial waters.

I come from a time and a part of the world where class distinctions were very clear. In beholding Christ in Nazareth, in that lowly social class, my Russian heart and mind filled with joy. This lowly human estate of the Son of God revealed the immense love of God for me. By assuming that condition of a worker-peasant, he identified himself with the lowest of mankind. He did that because he loved us so, especially the poor. In Russia, incidentally, even with all its social and class stratification, love for the poor was very great because of what Christ had done for us.

Moreover, I had in my own family living examples of these ideas.

My mother, as I have mentioned, was a talented concert pianist. During her undergraduate years at the conservatory of St. Petersburg, she "went to the people" every summer. This means that she hired herself out for a few rubles, as a maid to just the type of people that Joseph and Mary were—worker-peasants.

This movement of "going to the people" had been started by the intellectuals of Russia. In many cases, aristocratic members of the intellectual elite became farmhands and taught "letters" to the peasants. It was done incognito, that is to say, some excuse was given for doing these things. My mother dressed in the peasant costume of the poor and presented herself as a maid for hire. She knew more than the average person, and worked very hard at many tasks. Often she served the poor as a nurse. Her father was a doctor, so she had some medical knowledge.

Her days were strenuous. She got up early, helped with the cleaning, prepared the breakfast, did the washing all by hand, went on with the chores of the day, prepared lunch and dinner, cleaned—whatever this peasant family needed. When she returned in the fall she had succeeded in teaching the whole family how to read and write.

Naturally, her hands suffered. When her teacher saw the state of her hands, he exclaimed in horror, "Pianists' hands shouldn't look like that!" But mother said, "Wait a minute and

181

listen." Then she began to play. All her experience of having gone to the poor, the deep cries of Russians whom nobody heard, was in her music. It was beautiful. She added, "Cold cream will take care of my hands!"

My mother had revolutionary ideas, in the Christian sense. She believed that all Christians must love one another! She translated this love into direct action by personal counseling, interest and involvement with other people, but especially by involvement with the poor.

Early in life she indoctrinated me into identification with Christ in the poor. I grew up knowing this truth with my heart.

As soon as I was old enough, she involved me in these works of mercy. I would put a pack on my back, filled with medicine and other supplies, and journey with her sometimes as much as 70 miles (usually only about 10 or 20, but sometimes farther). We would sleep in huts along the way. When we reached our destination, the first thing I had to do was scrub the floor, clean the utensils she would be needing, fix the beds, and generally make myself useful. Then I prepared the food for the family because often the woman was in labor. Mother attended to this, and I attended to all the rest. It was quite something, believe me.

Occasionally she allowed me to participate in some of her work, like the care of the baby after it was born. But then, she not only delivered babies; she did all kinds of medical work. I did the best I could and learned a great deal. Then we would trudge back the many miles we had walked. She would say, "Well, that wasn't too bad, was it?" I would answer, "Oh no, it was wonderful!"

I learned to be, shall we say, merciful to the poor. In those days, ladies and gentlemen didn't exactly do those things: at least, none of our neighbors did. They all thought mother was slightly crazy. The memory of these trips is deeply embedded in my mind.

I could tell you hundreds of stories about the Christian generosity of my father and mother, but what I wish to emphasize here is the connection between nature and grace. I think that the reasons which motivated my parents in their Christian lives also inspired my own vocation. I have always attributed my vocation, at least in part, to my parents, especially my mother. She went to the poor, went to the people, because like other Russians she felt herself a member of the Mystical Body. Every Russian keenly felt this oneness with all Christians. Experiencing also a deep sense of sin, he wished to atone by acts of this kind.

Social service, as known in the Western world, was almost nonexistent in my country. There were few orphanages or old people's homes. Beginning with the social unit of the village, and going up the ladder to the higher social units of the aristocracy, the people felt that the words of Christ—"Whatsoever you do to one of these . . ."—applied to orphans and old people. Therefore, no one wanted to get rid of orphans or old people. Either the family kept the children, or strangers would take them in. Likewise with the elderly. Old age was revered and catered to, as it was a symbol of wisdom.

This was my spiritual formation regarding the poor. Eventually it resulted in Russian spirituality at work in the slums of Toronto. Perhaps that was one of the reasons God brought me to that strange city, in many ways so inimical to everything I stood for. But who knows the ways of God! The same spirituality was at work in Harlem, and is now at work here in Combermere.

Upon the death of my father, my mother found among his books one which she had never seen before. On the flyleaf was written: "My debt to God." He listed the things he considered his debt to God. He had sponsored many people through college. He had an interest in what today are called "detox" centers. He gave dowries, like St. Nicholas, to girls who couldn't marry because they were too poor. Yes, the list of father's "debt to God" was rather long.

I thought all parents were like mine, but now I know better. Not for a moment did they ever neglect to instill gospel attitudes in me. In my organization of the apostolate, I used the ideas and patterns I had learned from my parents. In my books I describe this spirituality of Madonna House, and how the ideas and inspiration of my parents took on flesh in Combermere over the years.

1974, foundress and guiding light
of Madonna House

16. The Age of Vatican II

Since this book contains only vignettes from my life, and makes no pretension of completeness, I pass over the next few years at Madonna House and arrive at the late 50s and early 60s. Madonna House became a little microcosm of the church, experiencing many of the phases occurring in the church at large.

First came the age of psychiatry, and the need to unite psychiatry and religion. One day, coming out of church, I accidentally met Dr. Karl Stern. He invited me to tea and we began talking.

Very, very gently he said, "Catherine, you must acquaint your staff with emotional problems."

I said, "Doctor, I have only minimal training in psychiatry, less than a year."

He said, "That's not important, Catherine, you are being trained by God. I would go to you for counseling myself." (He did later on.) "You are a very wonderful psychiatrist after experiencing Toronto, Harlem, and all your years of listening to people. I'll back you up."

I agreed to begin.

Dr. Stern approved of my way of teaching. He often visited Combermere and we had wonderful talks. I began to experience the transfers, the hostilities and the like. I had realized the need for a marriage between psychiatry and religion but, alas, the way was not smooth. Few psychiatrists at that time were trying to establish this relationship, but I did my best to connect the two.

I gave it up after some years. I decided I was not really qualified, although I could still see a great need for this kind of counseling in the church. Still, I started a trend. Our staff and many other people ceased to be afraid of psychiatry or ashamed of it, and that helped. I thought that the church should be in the forefront, but it is taking her time to catch up.

Out of this trend another difficulty arose: Everybody wanted to be a counselor. Many priests wanted to become psychiatrists to fulfill their own needs instead of helping the church as God wanted. Even to this day I pray for a fruitful marriage between the church and psychiatry. It seems as though God has taken me by the hand and said, "Catherine, let us just walk a little ahead of everybody else, eh? I'll show you what my church needs."

Then came Vatican II and its aftermath. Some years before I had thought chaos had reached its culmination, but I was gravely mistaken. It had only begun! Something went nutty in the church. The devil was spreading neuroses all over. Priests thought they had to become "relevant." Relevant to what? To whom? Suddenly people came to see me because I had been in Harlem. Suddenly the things for which I had been condemned became the "in" things.

Before Vatican II, I had seen the necessity of stability for an effective lay apostolate. In Harlem, a little Negro boy cried because his white volunteer friend only stayed three months. He said that she was the first white person he loved—and she went away! At the time, I didn't know anything about secular institutes, but I began to write about the need for stability. I thought and prayed about the necessity of taking a vow of stability. The church needed a laity that was stable. Lo and behold, that's what the future pope, Cardinal Montini (Pope Paul VI), told me in 1951. Shortly after that I wrote a constitution and established such a stable community. Again, God had showed me ahead of time what to do.

Thus, when the renewal hit the religious orders, people by the thousands began to come to Combermere to see men and women living in chastity. While nuns were jumping over the walls and priests were getting married, a group of lay people lived peacefully (comparatively speaking!), attending to its business. Some priests joined us. In a sense, God seemed to be walking several steps ahead of events through me, and presenting our community as some kind of model.

Next, the hippies came on the scene. I pondered, "There must be an apostolate to these people. We should be among them." But the demands of the apostolate did not allow us the opportunity. Once again God arranged things. The Bishop sent me to a theological conference in Toronto.

Walking out of a meeting at the University of Toronto, I came upon a group of hippies sleeping and lying on the grass. One girl stopped me and asked, "Are you a nun without a habit?" (She had seen my silver cross shining in the sun.) I said, "No, I'm a person."

Well, I must have pushed the right button on the right hippy! She jumped up and began shouting to everybody, "Come here! Come here! I found a person! She's an adult, but she's a person!"

I must admit I was flabbergasted, but the ways of God are inexplicable. She said, "Sit down." So I sat down. She said, "Do you know J.C.?" (J.C., I knew, was Jesus Christ.) I just looked at her—she was young, a real hippy—and said, jokingly, "Do I know J.C.? Do I know J.C.? Sister, if you were an astronaut going to the moon in a rocket, I'd pass you by as if you were a milk train!"

Forty pairs of huge eyes just looked at me. The queries began: "LSD?" "Marijuana?" "Horse?" I said, "Are you trying to ask me if I take drugs to get to J.C.? You are absolutely infantile. You don't get to J.C. on drugs. It's a sin to take drugs. Though J.C. loves sinners, he doesn't love the drugs that spoil his creation which is your bodies. For Pete's sake!" (I really got mad!)

"Well, then," they asked, "how do you reach J.C.?" I thought of the words of scripture, "Let the little children come to me." For 10 days, four hours a day—first 40, then 50, then 100, then 200 hippies—I talked to them about Teresa of Avila, Francis of Assisi, St. John of the Cross. I read to them from Francis Thompson's *Hound of Heaven*. I spoke to them of the Russian saints, the desert Fathers, and Elizabeth of the Trinity.

Their eyes grew bigger. "We thought Zen did that." I said, "Zen is okay, the Buddhists are okay. The Lord is leading them to himself by a different way. But you wanted to meet J.C. This is the way you do it."

When I was about to leave they said, "Look, we have a clean room, a new mattress, a table and chair. Everything is quite comfortable. Why don't you come and stay with us? You could be our guru." I said, "Sorry, I'm already a guru someplace else." (This was my Russian humor coming out, but they didn't know it!)

Well, I departed, without giving them my address. Foolishly, I thought they wouldn't be able to find it. Just a week later, two men and two girls appeared on the scene. They said, "We found your guru place." I said, "I guess you did." Fortunately one of our priests was around. I was busy, so I said to them, "Now there's a real guru. You go and listen to him."

The next thing I knew, many communes sprang up in the district. I'm not saying they all came because of me, but they did follow those first four people. For about 10 years they came to Madonna House in droves. I realized that this was an apostolate in itself. I opened the doors wide, exposing myself and the community to a lot of trouble with the Mounties and everybody else, because they were part of the drug scene.

However, they were considerate, They didn't use drugs on our premises. In fact, one of the young girls who was staying with us went through the visitors' jeans! When she found drugs, she threw them in the Madawaska River. And when a known (known to them!) pusher arrived, they said, "Not here. Don't do it. The Mounties are too close, just around the corner." So he departed. Our visitors protected us!

Quite a few of these hippies became converts; many of them left the drug scene. I had once hoped to start coffeehouses in various locales among them. Instead, they came to us. Once more the Lord had taken me by the hand and pulled me ahead of everybody else. The result was a greatly extended and personalized apostolate. I had friends in San Francisco, Vancouver, Hawaii, Toronto and many other cities. Many a distraught mother or father telephoned me asking that I locate a missing child through my contacts with the hippies.

This became a part of the apostolate of Madonna House. Our staff just accepted the hippies and took everything in stride. But I must admit that a wound in my heart grew bigger. I realized there was a breakdown of family life. It wasn't changes in the liturgy—the guitar Masses and such—that really captivated these young people. Truth captivated them: They were seeking the truth. Some traveled all the way to India in search of this truth. They gave up drugs to practice Zen Buddhism.

Where was the church in all this? Where were we, the people of God? We seemed to be fast asleep. A girl, a student at a Catholic college, told me she had slept with 48 different men! I wonder what the Catholic college was doing about it all. She said,

"You understand: I can talk to you. You are the first person I have been able to speak to about this." She is a Carmelite now, and I receive letters from her.

Another visitor was leading the life of a prostitute in order to acquire drugs. Now she has graduated from a college and leads a normal life. The examples are endless. Yes, the Lord took me by the hand and said, "These are the needs of my church. Do something!" I did. He always seems to open a curtain part of the way and then says, "Now do this."

Next came the call to the foreign missions. I have always been mission-minded. That's why I fought the staff's decision to limit the apostolate to only Negroes when I was in Harlem. I said, "I didn't come here to work in a paternalistic way with the Negro. Our vision must be worldwide. Combermere is the next step." Thus we have set up Madonna House missions in Bangladesh, Peru, Honduras, the West Indies, and Israel.

In the early sixties the church appeared to be in chaos, to be going over some kind of precipice. It seemed to be dissolving. But I knew, with a faith that nothing could shake, that the powers of hell would never prevail. Nothing seemed to affect my faith, the powerful faith that God had given me. It became a sort of pivot around which young people began to gather. Something of the deep faith that God had endowed me with penetrated those hippies, those young people. Faith in the church, faith in the Lord, faith in our Lady. I discerned in my soul that this was the moment of faith.

But I was sorely tried; in fact, tried by fire. I have had much pain in my life, but where are the words to explain the kind of pain which suddenly, like a sword, entered my soul? Often I thought of our Lady and the many swords which pierced her heart. Because I loved her so, perhaps in a small manner they entered mine as well.

There were moments when I would hang on to Mary's garments even as the woman with the issue of blood clung to Christ's garments. Mary was like me: she was a creature. That made her kin to me. I cannot explain how, but it was as if during those horrible years I constantly threw myself into her arms. She seemed to be the one who could understand and console me.

I wrote many poems about her. Then one day, I understood. Again, God pulled aside the curtain which veiled his mysteries. I understood that I was being given the dead Christ as he had been given to Mary, for the church had suddenly entered a strange era. It didn't last too long, but everybody started talking about the "death of God." An Anglican bishop wrote and asked the question, "Is God dead?" The idea spread. The devil blew the little flame into a huge bonfire. People came to us by the hundreds asking, "Is God really dead?"

I thought of Mary holding his body. She knew, though it might have been a mystery to her also, that he would rise from the dead. I knew he would too. But they kept throwing the dead Christ into my lap, and I kept singing lullabies to him because I knew he wasn't dead. I knew he was only sleeping in the hearts of those people. I sang him a Russian lullaby:

> Sleep, beloved child of mine. Sleep,
> little mite. Sleep while there is time.
> Very soon, very soon, you will be called
> into battle, and before you know it, you
> will grow up. I will have to embroider
> your saddle with silver and with wool.
> But not yet. Sleep, little child. Sleep,
> little mite, before life will call you to
> its battle.

I sang thus to him in my heart the same lullaby my mother sang to me, though nobody heard me singing.

Nevertheless, there is something very important here that has to be understood: to hold the dead Christ even for a second is beyond all pain, because those who have thrown him in your lap have killed him. That was the tragedy.

I faced the death-of-God movement as it rolled in strong waves across the North American continent. I felt both weak and strong at the same time. The strength was not mine. The grace, the charism, as they say, of fighting for the church flowed into me. St. Joan of Arc fought; St. Catherine fought. In a sense, they were my patron saints. I prayed to them often during those years. I have both a statue and a relic of St. Catherine. I carried the relic on my person as the dead Christ—the death-of-God issue—was thrown at me. I knew that I was on guard for the church. To defend the church you have to be crucified, always crucified.

Then the priests started coming. I watched them. So many wanted to leave the priesthood. A society known as Bearings was established to help them find their "bearings" when they left the priestly ministry. Many people were interested in Bearings, but not so many were interested in keeping these priests in the church.

These waves of priests became like battering rams, tending to destroy the very notion of priesthood. They called themselves "presidents of the assembly" and other strange names. They refused to wear any kind of clothing which would distinguish them as priests—not even small crosses. They came around in stretch-pants which helped them cut fine figures but which were not becoming for priests. You wanted to weep at the sight of them. It seemed to me that they were trying to grab at the seamless robe of the church and tear it apart, to expose it as just another "organization" whose structures were obsolete. Everything became grist for their mills of criticism.

They spoke as if they were preaching, but it didn't come out as gospel. They spoke as if they knew what they were talking about, yet in their hearts they were not at peace. Something within me was crying out, "Stop! Stop!" I don't ever remember a pain quite so deep as the pain of meeting all those priests who wanted to leave the church, become laicized, or marry. But God worked on them through us.

For example, two girls about 17 and 18 were sitting at a table in the dining room drinking tea, and they seemed quite unhappy.

I said, "What's the matter with you? Are you as unhappy as you look?"

The 17-year-old said, "Oh, we've been misinformed. We were told that we could find a priest in Madonna House. We haven't been to confession in months because all the priests in Toronto are looking for their indemnity."

The 18-year-old said, " 'Identity,' not 'indemnity.' "

"Indemnity, identity . . . who cares! They are looking out for themselves. All we want them to do is hear our confessions, but we can't find them. They don't wear black anymore. How do we know who they are? We're scared to go to rectories. I don't see anybody here in black either."

Just then a young priest was passing by who had told me an hour or so before that he had made up his mind to ask his bishop for laicization. As he passed by I said, "Father, would you please hear the confessions of these young people?" If looks could kill, I would have been dead! But he was still a priest, and kids still have to go to confession. The kids looked at him imploringly. Then they went up together to the chapel over the large common room.

I sat there, thinking and praying about it all, when clump, clump, clump, down came the kids, bright-eyed, but no priest. So I went upstairs. Kneeling down with his face on the bench was my priest friend, crying. I handed him a big handkerchief and said, "Father, what's the matter?" He said, "Out of the mouths of babes . . . I realized that I cannot leave . . . not with kids like that around." I knelt beside him and thanked our Lady and the Lord. I left him alone with the big handkerchief.

That's only one story, I don't know how may priests remained in the priesthood because of Madonna House. Maybe our own priests could tell me. All I know is that in talking to me I represented something to them, and they knew that I loved them. They confided in me, asked my advice, discussed with me their most intimate personal problems. Many remained in the priesthood. They remained because Madonna House was there, stood firm, unshakable in its faith in God and in the church. Their letters to me bear witness to what happened to them.

Priests were getting involved in everything. They were going to the inner city, they were becoming psychiatrists, they wanted to do things we had been doing for years. Now these things were the rage. Hour after hour, day in and day out, I told them: "Please, give us the Eucharist, give us the sacraments, give us the word of God. We need you. We lay people can be the psychiatrists, we can go into the inner city. We can do many of these things. But we cannot do your work. Be priests for us. Why do you want to be somebody else?"

Night after night I sat with priests and nuns, explaining the obvious, the essentials, the very core of our faith. Yes, God chose me, and us of Madonna House, to be defenders of the faith in a very simple, direct (and often in my case blatant!) manner. I didn't lose my temper, but sometimes I had to use the words of Christ (which were not always gentle!) to bring them back to their vocations. I think we were successful in fighting for the church.

The nuns were worse that the priests. I spoke to 18 different groups on the renewal. One session lasted 10 days, and there were two sister-representatives from many of the major orders of the U.S.A. At first I felt like St. Stephen, experiencing a kind of verbal stoning. I couldn't understand how they dared do some of the things they did. Let me give you a few examples.

One of the major questions concerned religious garb. They were shedding their habits and switching to lay clothes. I experienced a powerful pain about all this. I love poverty. I have always thought of nuns as people who were poor, at least in the matter of clothes. But my heart wept over nuns curling their hair, wearing stockings, smoking, and wearing smart clothes. I don't think my heart wept for any group of people more than for these nuns. They were under vows of poverty, chastity, and obedience. Everything was going overboard. I reeled from it all.

Take another example. I was invited to speak at the chapter meeting of a highly respected order. The sessions consisted of a business meeting, followed by a spiritual talk. They conducted the business meeting, I delivered the spiritual talk. I seldom cry in public, but I cried when I heard these women discussing their vacations. They wanted the order to send them to Europe or any other place for purely recreational purposes.

For accommodations, I was given the "cell" of one of the sisters. The "cell" consisted of a 20- by 30-foot bedroom with an adjoining office, and next to the office a kitchenette, equipped with all the latest electrical gadgets. Of course, the refrigerator was filled with snacks of all kinds. I couldn't sleep in that suite. All night long I was up and down, up and down. Finally, in the morning light, I found the chapel, not far from my "cell." I slept there. They all had "cells" like that.

So I gave my talk. In the middle of it I suddenly put my head down on the lectern and began to cry. I sobbed and sobbed and sobbed. Then, feeling as if I had cords in my hands, I spoke. You have never heard such a lecture!

Afterwards the chaplain called me into his office and said, "Catherine, you weren't speaking to them, God was," and he kissed my hand. The Reverend Mother kissed me and said, "I don't think you need to stay any longer. It is going to take us a long time to absorb what you have said." There were happy results, thank God. Things changed for the better.

All during those years, and even now, we have nuns stay with us for various lengths of time. I don't know how much of an effect we have upon them. In the scriptures there is the account of Jacob wrestling with God face to face. That's how I felt sometimes—but

I wasn't wrestling with God. I was wrestling with the devil. I still
think so.

Here is what I think a nun should be:

>A nun is a woman
>Who believes in the Absolute,
>And arises in search of it,
>Laughing at all who
>Speak of the impossibility of it.
>For a woman, who is a nun,
>Knows that the impossible
>Becomes the possible
>In a matter of seconds,
>At the bidding of her Beloved.
>
>A nun is a woman who has become mad,
>Totally, irrevocably mad!
>For she has accepted
>The standard of God's wisdom
>Which is in truth folly to man.
>
>A nun is a woman
>Hanging on the other
>Side of his cross
>Knowing that it becomes
>His marriage bed with her
>The moment she asks
>"To be lifted up" with him.
>
>A nun is a woman
>Of the water and the towel
>Constantly kneeling before
>Mankind to wash its
>Tired feet.
>
>A nun is a woman
>In love with God—hence with all humanity
>Always . . . constantly . . . totally!
>
>A nun is a prayer—
>Everlastingly lifting her arms to God
>For those who don't.
>
>A nun is a woman
>Who fasts

Knowing well how fast fast reaches
The heart of God!

A nun is a woman
Wrapped in the
Poverty of God,
The mantle of
His surrender, his emptying!

A nun is a woman
Who exists
To show that God exists too.

Weakness and betrayals did not affect my love for priests and sisters. When they were arguing with me I felt like saying to them, as Christ had said to Peter, "John, Jack, Sister Anne, Sister Mary, do you love me? If you do, then feed my lambs." I never said it because it would have sounded too presumptuous.

Years ago Pope Pius XII had spoken prophetic words to me. It was only during the time of the Council that I realized just how prophetic they were. He said: "Madam, we need stable, dedicated lay people who will defend the church, who will restore the church, because the church is about to suffer again." (These may not be his exact words: I was so deeply moved as he was speaking.) But this is why our apostolate exists. He foresaw what would be needed in the church. Like our Lady, we said yes. We stood for years under the cross of Christ. That's why we hold on to Mary. She knew what it was to stand there.

1978, honorary degree

17. The Church and I

I have always loved the church. This is a very strange statement to make: All Christians should love the church. But from earliest childhood I have had a deep, deep feeling for her. As a child it made no difference to me whether the church building was Orthodox or Roman Catholic. The building itself attracted me. I didn't understand then too much about the church as the Mystical Body of Christ. It was the building itself that held a fascination. Time and again I would just walk in and sit down. Sometimes I collected flowers and strewed them in front of the iconostasis or the Holy Doors. In a Catholic church I used to climb the altar steps and lay flowers in front of what I called the "Little House."

Now that I am thinking about it, my son George used to do the same thing. He used to take his toys to St. Basil's Church in Toronto (we lived right across the street) and place them in front of the tabernacle. Nobody knew who kept doing this, but the sacristan had to keep removing them. One day he caught George "in the act." The sacristan crossed the street to inform me of what was happening; also to return all the toys. When my son saw the toys returned, he said, "Oh, God sent them back! I must give him some new ones!" Did my son inherit this custom from me? Who can tell. All I know is that from an early age I loved the church building itself, and so did my son.

When I was a small girl I didn't know very much about the way of the cross, but I loved to walk along and follow the pictures. I was always very sorry that Jesus Christ had had such a tough time! I remember once collecting all the crucifixes my mother had and taking Jesus off each one! In school I remember using a small ladder to reach the bloody feet of Jesus. I scrubbed the red paint off! The sisters were terribly incensed, and wanted to know who had done it. They gathered all the children and asked, "Who did it?'' In front of everybody I walked up and said, "I did." They asked why. I said, "I couldn't stand to see him with all those nails and all that blood. I just wanted to make him more comfortable." I wasn't punished!

I discovered that my father also loved the church building.

When I was growing up in St. Petersburg I always walked from school to home with my governess. I liked to stop in at St. Isaac's Cathedral. One day, there, in front of our Lady's icon, was my father. He stayed there for two hours. I know because I wanted to find out how long he prayed and I stayed until he walked out! My governess was very annoyed with me for staying so long, but she couldn't say very much. After all, I *was* in church, and there was my father doing the same thing! I wasn't even 10 years old at the time.

As my father was walking out I asked him what he was doing there so long. He said, "Catherine, I do what everybody else does in church—pray." All this impressed me very much. Perhaps this experience helped to make the church building attractive to me. I sensed what people call a "presence" in the church, and it held a very deep attraction for me. Through it, God was laying in me the foundation for something else.

As I grew up I began to understand the *Christian* idea of the church. I began to realize who and what the church was. I saw that the church was the spotless bride of Christ. I saw her clad in the king's robes, beautiful and glorious. This vision stayed in my heart like a warm, consoling thought: The church was the spotless, shining, radiant bride of Christ. I applied to the church that beautiful passage from the psalms, "The king's daughter is decked in her chamber with gold-woven robes: in many-colored robes she is led to the king" (Ps 45:13-14). The church was something holy, precious, something you should even give your life for.

In Canada I discovered that the church was the people of God. It took me a long time to understand that the people of God was the Mystical Body of Christ, and that Christ was the head of this body. Why didn't I understand? Because of sin, the terrible sins of the people of God. I was torn by a contradiction: This sinless bride of Christ was also the sinful bride of Christ! How could that be? It took me a long time to understand a very simple thing—that Jesus came to reconcile us sinners with his Father.

As Dostoevsky wrote, "He loved man in his sin." God had rescued man from his sin. The whole picture of the church was now completed for me. I understood something else: The sin of one member of the church was the sin of all, that is, if I sin, I affect the whole church.

Life eventually became for me a throbbing pain. I was torn by the sins of others. I can't explain it. I think I began to experience this when I experienced the ruins of church buildings.

I have seen more ruined churches perhaps than anyone else. I described how I saw them in Russia, in Spain, and in Germany. Many of them now have been restored, but I have never forgotten the "presence" I felt as a child, and how I experienced this presence even in a ruined church. I saw people pray in ruined churches. They had caught a glimpse of what a church really was, and they turned toward him who even dwelt amidst the ruins.

The liturgy for the dedication of a church begins with the words, "This place is awesome (terribilis)." Even outside the liturgical ceremony I experienced the meaning of that word. Whether standing in front of "happy" churches (in good condition), or in front of ruined churches, I have experienced in my body the awesomeness of the church's spiritual nature. It has shaken my whole being. At those moments I understood why the Lord calls himself the bridegroom. I can't explain it. But I understood one glorious day that he was my bridegroom, and that I was part of his people, part of his flock, part of his Mystical Body. I understood the mystical notion of the nuptials of the Christian with his God. Because I entered into this mystery of love, I entered into the mystery of the church. I still live in this mystery.

When a person falls in love with God, then the church becomes a reality of faith. This cannot be explained rationally. The head must enter into the heart, close its eyes, and adore a reality which can only be embraced in faith. I walked into that reality, that mystery, not knowing that I was walking in faith.

I have written a book called The Unknown Mysteries of Our Lady.[1] In these poems I expressed in a small way the pain in which I walked as I grew in an understanding of who and what the church is.

---

[1] Dimension Books, Inc., 1979.

To walk into the mystery of the church is also to walk into the mystery of the priesthood. The priest, whether he wishes to acknowledge it or not, is Christ. Before Jesus ascended into heaven, he gave us the church so that we would not be orphans. He also gave us the Eucharist, the mystery which keeps the church alive. He left us the Eucharist so that we might feed on him. This is one of the most fantastic mysteries of all. No wonder that so many of his disciples left him when he said, "Unless you eat the flesh of the Son of Man and drink his blood, you shall not have life in you." They left because they didn't understand the language of a Lover.

The simplest things that a man could give his friends were bread and wine. Christ made these elements a vehicle of his love, of his strength, so that his followers could live his law of love. It is in the mystery of the Eucharist that we acquire the strength to live this law of love.

Yes, Christ is the bridegroom, and every man and woman is his bride—all men and women together. He wishes to introduce each one of us to his Father. It is through the bread and wine that God and myself became one. It's a mystical union. No headwork is required. It must simply be accepted in faith. He who drinks his blood and eats his flesh becomes known to the Father in the most intimate fashion, as the bride becomes known to the husband.

From the very beginning of my apostolate, when I sold all that I had, God gave me a tremendous love for the church and for priests. This church cannot perish. When you love the church, you even love those in the church who do evil. You know that over the centuries the church has been ruined over and over again, and each time she has risen anew more splendid than ever. God has given me an overpowering love for the church. Call me a fool. I am a fool. I see Christ in the church.

All along my journey, God gave me, I think, the gift of insight and foreknowledge concerning the church. From day to day, I always seem to see a little bit of what the church is presently undergoing and where she is headed. I always know that she will endure. I used to doubt this gift because it is very painful.

When those three young women and two young men came to join me in the early days of Toronto, when I had left my poustinia to start this lay apostolate, I realized then that we were living in troubled times. A stark economic depression was crippling the whole world. I always connected current events with the church in the sense that my first reaction to news would be, "How is this going to affect the church?" From my earliest days in the apostolate I said to myself, "We have to renew the church."

As I near the close, now, of these vignettes from my life, I want to review how the Lord took me by the hand and led me step by step, anticipating the needs of the church.

The first need was that of poverty. I knew that whatever we did as a little group, we must be beggars, because so many people in the church were rich. I did not know, at that time, of the wealth of the orders, but I surmised it. I sensed that St. Francis had the real answer before Brother Elias weakened his work by building all those monasteries. I felt that our apostolate too had to be Franciscan, but in a very modern Franciscan way, allowing for great freedom and with practically no structures.

In 1930 this was not the thing to do! It was rebellion. Only Archbishop Neil McNeil understood what I had in mind, and he covered me with the mantle of his office so that I was able to survive. I did survive, but I want you to know that I lived on the edge of a precipice. Eventually I was forced out of Toronto by public pressure. The words of Father Carr at that time still ring in my ears: "They hate you because you are doing what they should be doing."

The next need within the church was for some people to identify with the poor. Some of its members had to be identified with the poor for the spiritual well-being of the whole church. The notion that came into my head was the use of storefronts. You cannot be paternalistic toward the poor, that is, live somewhere else and just drop in once in a while and do some kind of social work. You have to become poor. Identification with the poor is identification with Jesus Christ. True, he did say that "the poor you will always have with you." But he also said, "I was in prison . . . I was hungry, etc." We cannot forget this judgment that awaits us. I pondered very seriously that judgment.

Again, this kind of thinking was radical and unique. We were pioneers. Women just didn't live in storefronts with hoboes! Certainly not! However, it worked! It worked for the hoboes, and it worked for the many, many people who came to join us. I understood that begging and being one with the poor was (and always will be) a crying need of the church.

Poverty, identification with the poor. Then, because I was lecturing and constantly being questioned by everyone, I recognized the need to *live by the gospel.* I possessed a New Testament which I carried with me at all times. The only answers I gave people were from the gospel, from the scriptures. I realized then that what the church, the people of God, needed was the strong food of the Holy Scriptures. All those intellectual sermons, so prominent in those days, were getting the church nowhere.

I also realized deep down in my heart that the promotion of all the novenas and devotions was not the answer either. Oh, there is nothing wrong with novenas, First Fridays, First Saturdays and the rest. I am all for those things. I am all for them, *provided* they do not take the place of the liturgy and the scriptures. So I started teaching the liturgy and the scriptures, because these were crying needs of the people of God.

Fathers Godfrey Diekmann and Virgil Michel were doing the same thing. I forgot how many people attended the first liturgical conference. Forty or so. You were laughed out of house and home for going. Teaching scripture! Nobody taught scripture, only priests to seminarians. You weren't even supposed to *read* the scriptures! I didn't care. Even if they crucified me, I didn't care. With the help of these two good Fathers I continued teaching the liturgy and the scriptures, always with the approval of the bishop.

But the pain was growing. It appeared to me that I was becoming one immense wound. I kept praying. I began to realize that anyone who accepts the gospel without compromise will not only become a wound, but a wound into which many people will constantly pour salt.

Years later in Harlem I sensed another need of the church: martyrdom. The church needed—not big, spectacular martyrs but—little martyrs, little beggars, poor people to live with the poor. The church needed people to teach the gospel and the liturgy in order not to compromise the gospel. This is what it means to be little martyrs. Many people who worked with us were martyrs. They were persecuted even by their parents and friends. This was an anticipation of the future. Because today, all over the world, the church is being called to martyrdom.

Then came Hiroshima, the Bomb. I reviewed my history of the church and of the world. I concluded: "There have never been times such as these." As usual, the Lord gave me some kind of insight as to the meaning of these events for the future. In my heart I knew that Hiroshima spelled chaos for the world. Compared to Hiroshima, the Tower of Babel was child's play.

I began to watch people. What effect did Hiroshima have on them? Do you know what effect it had? It stirred up an incredible fear in people's unconscious. It stirred up a terrible anger against God and against the people who had created this chaos. Even those most unaware of the meaning of events knew that something had happened in the history of the world that had never happened before: The Bomb. People began to doubt the power of God to control the world. It seemed that the devil had won. Once again it seemed that the church too would be ruined. Once again someone had to lay down his life to prepare for the resurrection. I did. Many others did too.

Is it possible to bring you who read this into the very depths of my heart? Is it possible for you to understand? Will I ever be able to put into words the pain in my heart over the suffering of the church and of the world? Can I ever show you the wounds in this heart of mine? I feel like saying to you, "Have you ever seen a sorrow like unto my sorrow?" Of course, this is presumptuous—but my sorrow was great considering the smallness of my heart! Yes, come into my heart, my friends, and enter my sea of pain for the church, for the Holy Father, for priests, for the spotless bride of Christ, for the world. I have wept for them; now I place them in the hands of the Lord.

What is the final answer to this new barbarism which has entered the world? Once again, as I did in those early days in Toronto, I prostrate myself, Russian style, on various dirty floors. I realize now, as I did then, that the church needs prayer, for this is the time of the shaking of the foundations of the world.

My nights are once again vigils of God. Vigils are strange things, my friends. They come from God. He wakes you up and you become wide awake, The hour of the night matters not. It was in a recent vigil that I understood this is the time for prayer. Nothing else will do. Nothing else can stem the barbarism of a secular world busy worshiping itself and not caring about anything or anybody except its own satisfaction and gratification.

Once upon a time God wrote on a wall for a pagan king,

"MENE-TEKEL-PERES." It may be good to recall the interpretation of those words: "God has numbered your kingdom and put an end to it: you have been weighed on the scales and found wanting: your kingdom has been divided and given to the Medes and the Persians" (Dn 5:26-28—NAB). Today, on the walls of every nation, one can see and read the anger of God. The anger of God is really his mercy. But he is angry at us for shoving him away, for throwing him out of our world, for flaunting his laws. His anger is falling now upon us in many ways, national disasters of all kinds.

His anger also reveals us to ourselves. We see how much we kill, how much we hate, how much we are willing to batter others just to get our own way. We step on the heads of others just to climb a little higher ourselves.

One night (many years ago now), realizing that prayer was needed, I entered my past. (I go to my past in order to discern the future.) Out of my past came the remembrance of the poustinia (a Russian word for desert). I wrote a book about it. Poustinias have now spread all over the world. I hope they continue to do so. A poustinia is not a house of prayer, it is just a spot—a cabin, a room—where people can go to be alone for a day or so. If you wish to know more about it, I suggest you read my book.

I wrote *Poustinia*[2] to call people to the desert of prayer where they can face themselves and experience a change of heart. In the poustinia, *kenosis* (the Greek word for "empty") takes place, a stripping of oneself, a burying of the "I." In the poustinia we begin to live more for the other as Christ taught us, loving in depth both those who love us and those who hate us. "Greater love has no man than he lay down his life for his friends."

Night followed night, vigil followed vigil. I began to understand that Christ was seeking the disintegration, not of the church which will survive, but of secularism, of paganism, of the hedonism which at this present moment dominates the world. I began to understand that prayer is needed to counteract the spread of atheism which is slowly creeping over Portugal, Italy, France and England, countries that are becoming a prey to communism.

I saw the immense continent of Africa. I saw white people

---

[2]Ave Maria Press, 1975.

who professed to believe in a God who died for *all* mankind living in apartheid. They needed prayer. Yes, what the world needed was the power of the poustinia.

I slept. My nights were quiet for a while. Then the vigils started again. Something besides prayer was needed. He also told us to serve one another: "I have come to serve." The vigils increased, and out of them a new book came forth, *The Gospel Without Compromise.*[3] Service to one another was joined with prayer. Again I slept.

The vigils began once more, and I listened. A new word (but again, from my past) came to me: *Sobornost.*[4] Sobornost is the Russian word for "unity." The Lord prayed for unity—"That they might all be one, as you are in me and I am in you."

Words kept coming. *Strannik,*[5] the Russian word for "pilgrim." These three concepts formed a kind of spiritual triology. You enter the poustinia, the desert of your heart, to meditate on sobornost, the unity which we are called to achieve with God and with one another. When in the desert of our hearts we finally accept this solution of sobornost, it is then time to open the doors of our poustinia and journey forth as a strannik, as a pilgrim, to preach this good news to others.

These vigils of mine that have brought forth these books are times of prayer, because prayer is now the last resort. We have forgotten how to pray. We have forgotten that there must be a time when we are silent so we can hear what God wants to say to us. Yes, my friends, we must pray. It must be the prayer of two people in love with each other who cease to talk. Their silence speaks. This is the kind of prayer that the poustinia will teach you. Resting in God's love, you will understand the sobornost, the unity, he wishes for his children. Then, as a strannik, a pilgrim, you will go forth and shout and sing about this to all peoples.

Two people in love! When you are in love with God you will understand that he loved you first. You will enter into a deep and mysterious silence and in that silence become one with the Absolute. Sobornost! Your oneness with God will overflow to all your brothers and sisters.

My friends, this is the kind of prayer we need today. If you

---

[3]Ave Maria Press, 1976
[4]Ave Maria Press, 1977.
[5]Ave Maria Press, 1978.

pray like this you will be overshadowed by the wings of a dove, the symbol of the Holy Spirit. On those wings your prayer of silence will be lifted into the hands of the Woman Wrapped in Silence, and she will lay it at the feet of the Most Holy Trinity. The answer today to the salvation of mankind lies in prayer.